While the Iron is Hot

While the Iron is Hot
An Autobiography

Bernhard Langer
with Bill Elliott

Stanley Paul
London Sydney Auckland Johannesburg

Stanley Paul & Co. Ltd

An imprint of Century Hutchinson Ltd

62-65 Chandos Place, London WC2N 4NW

Century Hutchinson Australia (Pty) Ltd
89-91 Albion Street, Surry Hills, NSW 2010

Century Hutchinson New Zealand Limited
PO Box 40-086, Glenfield, Auckland 10

Century Hutchinson South Africa (Pty) Ltd
PO Box 337, Bergvlei 2012, South Africa

First published 1988
© Bernhard Langer 1988

Set in Century Schoolbook

Printed and bound in Great Britain by
Anchor Brendon, Tiptree, Essex

British Library Cataloguing in Publication Data

Langer, Bernhard
  While the iron is hot: an autobiography.
  1. Golf. Langer, Bernhard
  I. Title   II. Elliott, Bill
  796.352′092′4

ISBN 0 09 171200 9

Contents

Acknowledgements

The author would like to thank Bill Elliott for all his help in producing the manuscript. The publishers wish to thank Phil Sheldon, Matthew Harris, Peter Dazeley, Lawrence Levy and AllSport for permission to reproduce their copyright photographs.

1

A Master golfer at last...

Augusta in April. A Sunday morning. Like almost every Sunday morning in this small Georgia town the day blossomed early, the sunshine creeping across the Augusta National golf course to illuminate every nook and cranny, each dogwood and azalea of this sporting cathedral. It was the final day of the 1985 United States Masters and in houses and hotel rooms throughout Augusta golf fans were waking up and continuing the arguments from the night before: who was going to win the 49th Green Jacket to be put up for grabs in this the first major tournament of the year? No one's mind was concentrated more on this subject than Bernhard

Langer's as he woke after a fitful night's sleep in the pleasant house he rented through Masters week for himself and his American wife, Vikki. There was no rush to get out of bed as the German's eyes flicked open on to one of the most important days of his life. He was not to tee off until close to two o'clock. As one of the leaders after three rounds this was his advantage. As a professional golfer and a man determined to squeeze the most out of an extraordinary talent for hitting a ball round a manicured field he knew that what he had to do that Sunday morning was to occupy his mind, to keep at bay the dreams and the fear that dance together when a player is in with a chance of a truly glittering prize.

So after a breakfast that included the inevitable banana that he consumes each day to boost his potassium intake, Langer and his wife set off, as usual, for church that Sunday morning. As an enthusiastic Christian this was a perfectly normal thing for Langer to do. This special day, however, he wished to pray not only for others but also to ask for some divine assistance in achieving his goal that afternoon. Unfortunately for the Langers they found the local church inexplicably locked up when they arrived shortly before noon. It was scarcely a great omen. Yet even if someone had shut Bernhard out that morning, events were to show that someone else had decided to smile on him that day.

After finding the church locked, Vikki and I returned home where we prayed on our own. I say my prayers each day but that Sunday in a house that was neither my own nor God's was a special occasion. Throughout that week the conviction had grown within me that this was to be my time. I had already been close to winning the British Open on a couple of occasions but suddenly I felt confidence - real confidence - flooding through my body and my brain. All I needed was a little bit of luck.

At least what I didn't need was bad luck. So all I asked for that day was that I escaped any truly outrageous bad fortune. After that, if someone played better than me, so be it.

It is a wonderful feeling to be in with a chance of taking a major title - a mixture of nervousness and great anticipation. I couldn't wait to get started and to discover my fate that day; but over the years I had learned that I must stem my impatience, that I must force myself to be slow and methodical in my preparation. Once at the course, I knew that the adrenalin would flow freely enough. There was no need for me to try to turn on the tap prematurely. Indeed there is no need to try to get psyched up on such a day. The trick actually is to control your adrenalin, to use it to your advantage and not to allow it to control your actions.

But then just being at Augusta is exciting. It is the same whether you are a spectator or a player. It is a special place. And a special time. It marks the end of winter, the arrival of better weather and of better times. I first played there in 1982 and I fell in love with the occasion and the course immediately. For years I had watched the Masters on television and marvelled at the beauty of it all and wondered how I would cope with those fearsome greens. At one time when I was going through the worst of my putting problems only a crazy man or a fool would have dared to suggest that I was destined to win my first major title at such a place.

Masters week is one big party really. A lovely atmosphere; golf's equivalent to Wimbledon or Ascot. I felt as a player that I was part of a special kind of history every time I played there. The course actually is not that difficult: there is no real rough, the fairways are wide, the conditions usually perfect. Its difficulty lies in those greens and the fact that because the land rolls away from the clubhouse you have maybe two level lies per round, apart from when you are on the tee.

You must learn to know the place, to encourage it to embrace you. If you try too hard to attack it too quickly then you are dead. It calls for great subtlety, great shot-making. Put all these factors together and you have not only a great golf course but a great event. I've always felt that if you cannot get pumped up at the U S Masters then you must be clinically dead. Only the British Open can compete with Augusta for its tradition and atmosphere. There are four majors in the world but these two – the Masters and the British Open – are far ahead of the U S Open and the U S P G A, as far as this golfer is concerned.

As I drove to the club that day with Vikki I was already playing my final round inside my head. I was studying the pin positions that my caddy Peter Coleman had brought to me that morning and working out where I must try to land my tee shots to have the maximum chance of then placing my approaches correctly on the greens. Depending on where they cut those holes you can be better off 25 feet below the flag than four feet above it. Three putts are common at Augusta, four putts easy to come by.

But as my car turned into Magnolia Drive and the grand old clubhouse, which looks like a left-over from 'Gone with the Wind', came into view I rejected such negative thoughts. I felt great. I felt positive. Today I needed to draw on the experience I had gained from playing the 1982 and 1984 Masters, to learn from the mistakes I made back then and to build on those lessons for this last round.

In 1982 I had missed the halfway cut after finishing 11 shots behind the leader. At Augusta if you finish within 10 strokes of the leaders at the halfway point then you survive because in the Masters 10 shots is not as decisive with 36 holes left to play. But in 1982 I was confounded and bewildered by those greens. I had experienced nothing like them before. Of course I knew their reputation but the reality was frightening, like trying to walk barefoot on broken glass. I had slight putting problems in 1982 and in the 36 holes I played I had three-putted 11 times. It was a form of professional suicide.

In 1984 I did much better. I was learning, you see. As I loosened up on the practice ground with the other potential winners either side of me I was, like them, cocooned inside my own concentration. Not much is said at these times and what is said is instantly forgettable. Yet just 24 hours earlier it had looked unlikely that I would be in this pack of golfers hunting for one of the most coveted prizes in the game.

On the Friday night I was not being mentioned by any of the reporters as a possible victor. I was comfortably placed but not threatening. As usual on Friday night at Augusta a friend of mine, Harry Valerien, who works for German television, came round for dinner and to do an interview. I remember that he asked me if I was aiming to finish in the top 24 who automatically get invited back the following year. I surprised him by answering: 'No, Harry, I am aiming to win.' It must have seemed an outrageous statement to Harry at the time but I was serious – even if I did smile when I said it.

Then on the following day, after 12 holes of my third round, Harry must have been convinced that I was mad. By then I was two over par for the tournament and six shots behind the leaders. My chances of taking this Masters were disappearing faster than a racing car leaping off the starting grid.

I had hit my tee shot into the trees on the right of the 13th hole, a bad place on this famous par five. I looked at my lie, my stance, at the green that seemed to be grinning mockingly at me in the distance and said to myself, 'If you want to win this tournament then right here is where you have to get it going.' I asked my caddy for my three wood and I knew from the look in Peter Coleman's eyes that he thought I had lost my head. I didn't blame him. Anybody watching me must have thought the same. It was a ridiculous shot to attempt. It was not the club, but it was the time to take a chance. I knew I had 225 yards to the front edge of the green and I knew also that I usually hit my three wood 230 yards through the air. So if I could pull off a great shot I could just make it over Rae's Creek that guards the green and set up a birdie chance at least.

Instead I hit the ball thin. It shot off low, my eyes following it all the way, my heart sinking all the time. It was going to be short. I had no doubt about it. The ball finally bounced just in front of the creek, shot up in the air, cleared the water and bumped and rolled across the green, up the back and then came to rest 20 feet from the pin: I made the putt for eagle. My gamble had worked. I had found that little bit of luck every player needs. When I birdied the next two holes as well, I suddenly knew clearly that, yes, this could be my week.

I finished the third round two strokes behind Raymond Floyd, one adrift of Curtis Strange. More significantly, I was tied with Seve Ballesteros and so he and I had to play together in the final round. Significant because Seve is a difficult man to partner. It is not his fault, it is just his way. And there had been some bad publicity between us. The last time I had played with Seve was in the final of the World Matchplay Championship in England the previous year.

I had said that Seve intimidates opponents on the course and the Press had built this up into a major story before our match. It is true that I had said it but I had not realized the true meaning of the word. What I meant was that we were different sorts of people when we played. I like to be friendly, to talk with my partners during a round. Of course it is serious, but there is always time for a conversation in a four-hour round of golf. At least that is my way.

Seve, on the other hand, prefers to say little or nothing. He is so intense out there it is unbelievable. If he does not think it is a great - a truly great - shot he doesn't say anything. I find this attitude off-putting so I knew that this final round was, if anything, going to be tougher than ever because it was Seve and me. After all, he loves to win the Masters - almost expects to win the Masters - every time he plays there. His record, to be fair, suggests he is entitled to this opinion.

When we met on the first day and our names were announced, I knew only too well that most of the spectators saw me as nothing more than a supporting act to the Spaniard. They knew I was a very good player, of course, but was I good enough? Before we hit our opening drives, Seve and I shook hands and we wished each other good luck. Funnily enough we both meant it because, as I've suggested before, the one thing a golfer finds really difficult to cope with is rank bad luck.

I think the next time Seve spoke to me was 17 holes later as we stood on the 18th tee. So we began our final round. Two men, one from Spain, the other German, both trying to beat the best players America could put against us. And in their own backyard. The atmosphere was incredible. You could sense the expectations of the gallery as we knocked our drives down that first fairway. I recall thinking as I walked after my ball: 'Thank God it has begun at last.'

My game was simple in every way except its execution. Usually in golf - and always at the Masters - it is the guy who makes the fewest mistakes who triumphs on the final day. The front nine at Augusta can destroy a player if he is not very careful. There are no easy holes on this stretch. My plan had to be to survive these nine holes, then glance up and work out what I had to attempt over the back nine to win.

Despite the explosions of noise that greeted birdies from in front and behind me, I never once looked at a leader board. It was not until I stood on the 10th tee that I allowed myself to glance up to assess the situation. I was astonished. Curtis Strange had moved to seven under par for the tournament after picking up four shots on the front nine. It was impossible, surely, but Strange had done it, recovering brilliantly from his first round 80. I felt myself begin to crumble inside. Then I thought 'Well Langer - nobody cares whether you finish third or 10th or 25th. You want to win a major, so go for it; be aggressive, you have nothing to lose.'

So I threw away the caution with which I had covered the opening nine holes. Then came the ignition point as I parred the 10th - and on this killer hole that always feels like a birdie - parred the 11th, birdied the short 12th and birdied the 13th. I was rolling. It was happening. But was it enough? Then came the luck. Not good luck for me but bad luck for Strange. As he played the 13th he was in control of the tournament. It was his unless he did something wrong. He did. He hit his approach shot into Rae's Creek trying to set up a birdie chance and had to settle for a bogey. He was, however, still a stroke in front of me.

I heard the 'oohs' and 'aahs' that greeted his misfortune but I deliberately did not turn to look back. Instead I parred the 14th hole and then, as I stood on the 15th tee, a spectator shouted to me: 'You can win Bernhard, Curtis is blowing up.'

I wasn't sure what he meant exactly but I was still in an aggressive mood. I birdied the long 15th and parred the 16th. As I walked off that green, Strange was dropping a shot at the 15th and for the first time in my life I was in the lead at the U S Masters – by one stroke. Seve, meanwhile, was two shots behind me. Typically, he had nearly chipped in at the 16th for a birdie two and as he sank to his knees in despair after his ball refused to drop, my own heart soared. Every cloud, you know, has a silver lining for someone.

Seve, however, had not given up. I knew this only too well. The last two holes at Augusta are difficult enough if you are just playing them for fun. In the closing stages of the tournament they are minefields filled with potential disaster. When I birdied the 17th and he parred it, even Seve knew it was over for him. It was then as we stood together on the 18th tee that he spoke to me for the second time that day, tapping me on the back and saying: 'Well done, this is your week.'

That was very nice of him but first I had to make sure that I did not fall apart on this last uphill par four. I knew I had a two stroke lead but anything is possible and I still needed to muster all my concentration. I could not afford to begin relaxing yet. I hit a one iron off that last tee for safety because I needed to avoid the trees on the right and the bunkers on the left. Then I struck a four iron, aiming at the right-hand side of the green. Unfortunately, I hit it just six feet too far to the right and it flew into a bunker.

Still, I thought, no problem as long as it is not plugged. I hit a good bunker shot to six feet from the hole but read it outside left lip and the ball did not break at all. I had finished with a bogey five, my second dropped shot of the day. It was not a good finish but neither was it a disaster.

Seve shook my hand and put his arm round me. 'You are a great champion. You played really well,' he said. And he meant it. Apart from anything else, Seve loves to see Europeans beat Americans. He was disappointed at his own failure to grasp the prize but I could sense that he took a genuine pleasure in my success. Not that I had allowed myself yet to truly feel as though I had won. Curtis Strange had to play the last two holes. If he could make a birdie then I would be in a play-off. The only person who did not believe I had won was myself and, I am sure, Curtis Strange.

I had to keep myself tight, my concentration good, in case I needed to play on with him. Instead Strange dropped a shot at the last hole. I sat with my wife in the scorers' tent by the side of the green and when I saw his third shot at the last miss the hole I turned to Vikki, hugged her and said, 'I've done it, I am Masters champion.'

As ever, the next hour or so was hectic. I was driven away to the television people where I received my Green Jacket from the previous year's champion, Ben Crenshaw. I must say this famous coat looked a little odd on me as I was sporting red trousers and a red shirt at the time. Sartorially, I think I may have made a mistake that day but at least no one could accuse me of looking dull.

Then it was into the usual round of Press, radio and television interviews. The same questions, the same answers but, as always when you have won, good fun. Inevitably there is a swift feeling of anti-climax soon after such a victory. As the adrenalin leaves your system, so you go down. I knew what was going to happen, however, and so I was prepared for this depression. Usually it is 24 hours later when you truly begin to savour a big win. After the traditional dinner at the clubhouse, with all the members, Vikki and I set off for home shortly after 11 p.m. Instead of heading directly for our house I decided to make a detour.

Earlier that year, I had won the Australian Masters –

an event run by two typical Aussies, Frank Williams and David Inglis. On the eve of the US Masters Frank and David had gone to a calcutta evening which is a sort of auction where all the players are offered for purchase by the highest bidder. They had paid 3000 dollars to 'buy' me and friends had suggested they might have more fun watching their money burn.

Instead they had scooped the pool which was worth 96,000 dollars. I had won only a few thousand dollars more so I reckoned they owed me a drink at least. Instead of going home, we drove to their house where I knew a party would be in full swing. There I sat and drank some beer until about one o'clock. Then we headed home. We went straight to bed but could not sleep.

In truth I did not want to. Instead, I relived the day and what had happened. Like they say happens to a drowning man, my whole life flitted through my head. I thought of my parents and the people who had helped me get started; of the time I had nearly given up because of my putting problems; of the good times and the bad times that had helped to forge me as a person as well as a golfer; of the people who had helped me become what I am.

I thought, too, of Bill Rogers, the American golfer who won the 1981 British Open at Royal St George's, a championship I so nearly won myself. Poor Rogers had all but disappeared off the golfing scene by 1985, a man who somehow had his game destroyed by the greatest victory of his life. I wondered how that had happened – and why. I determined that it would not happen to me: that this Masters victory would be the real beginning of my career and not the end. Then as dawn broke over Augusta I finally fell into the deepest sleep of my life.

2

The beginning

Suddenly the train stopped. It was night and as the coaches trundled into one another Erwin Langer was jolted awake from a shivering sleep. Like everyone else aboard this particular train Erwin was tired and cold and hungry. He was also very frightened. The middle of Europe in September 1945 was not the place to be. The middle of Europe aboard a train carrying you and a few hundred other prisoners-of-war towards God knows what destination was an even worse place to be. For days now Langer and his companions had been herded together, told when to sit, when to stand and when to sleep. Not once had they been told exactly where they

*were heading or what their fate would be when they got
there. Even the most optimistic among them, however,
suspected that the end of the road might be just exactly
that. It was this destiny that Erwin Langer contemplated as he woke up this night on this train.*

*Of one thing he was certain – up to now fate had not
been overkind to him. Born in Sudetenland, now part of
Czechoslovakia but a German territory at the beginning of World War Two, Erwin's family were farmers.
He would have been a farmer himself had he not been
made a very special offer in 1938 when he was invited to
volunteer for the German Army. He could, of course,
reject this offer but the alternative was two years' hard
labour somewhere and then he would be conscripted
anyway. So he became a soldier.*

*By the time the war actually began he was a courier,
graduating from a bicycle to a motor-bike and then back
to a bicycle again before he was captured near Solingen
by the Russians. Erwin's capture was on 8 May 1945.
After several months in a POW camp, he heard he was
to be sent back to Czechoslovakia which by now was
under the control of the Russians. He had not heard
from his parents for a long time and was not even sure
that they were still alive. The prospect of returning to
his old homeland did not fill him with joy. Neither the
Russians nor the Czechs were inclined to extend the
hand of friendship to a German soldier and there were
rumours that the train would not stop at Sudetenland
anyway but head on towards some other alien and
awful destination.*

*For some reason the train's cargo of weary and
confused men was not guarded by the Russians but by
French soldiers who were less than diligent in their
task. As the train lumbered into motion again, Erwin
and several other prisoners decided to have a say in
their own fate. While the engine laboured up a hill a few*

miles short of the Czech border, Erwin jumped into the night and an unknown future. Over the winter months he scraped a living by working on remote farms for sympathetic farmers who gave him food and let him sleep in barns or other outbuildings. By April of 1946 he had made his way back to the Rhineland along with another ex-soldier. Though Erwin was reasonably sure that he would not be picked up and sent to Soviet-controlled Czechoslovakia any longer, he had to be careful to maintain a low profile just in case. Towards the end of April, however, he stepped out of the shadows long enough to learn that mail was once more being delivered between Germany and the Czechs. That evening he wrote to his parents' farm in Rabersdorf, Kreis Mährisch-Schönberg.

A month later, miraculously it seemed to Erwin, he received a reply. It was hardly reassuring. His parents told him that the Russians were throwing them out of the country, that the farm the family had tended for more than one hundred years, was no longer theirs. There had been no compensation, nothing. Like Erwin, they were virtually penniless. He was told to stay in Germany and that they would be in touch as soon as possible.

Towards the end of June he heard that his parents had made their way to Augsburg and were going on to Anhausen. It was there in September 1946 that Erwin became part of a family again. He also became a bricklayer.

In 1947 he met a local waitress named Wally and on 13 May 1949 they married. They lived more or less happily ever after and had three children, two boys and a girl. The youngest boy was born on 27 August 1957. Wally insisted they name their new son Bernhard.

My father has never glorified his dramatic escape from

the Russians. It is just a story he tells if he is asked but I like to think that I have inherited some of his strength of character, his determination to survive and to succeed. Certainly life was never easy for us as children in Anhausen. We were happy enough and we were loved but there was never a lot of money. In truth there was rarely much money at all. When I think back to the early days I seem to remember that my father was always working hard and my mother was always doing jobs too to earn a little extra money. It is why, I suppose, that I have not let the large amounts of money I now earn affect me too much. Maybe at times I have seemed a little too careful, but because of my childhood I appreciate the value of money and there has always been this little fear at the back of my mind that one day someone might come and take it all away from me. Only recently have I been able to rationalize this thought and to realize that, within reason, I can afford whatever I want for myself or my family. But back in Anhausen money was almost always a problem.

In truth it was because of the family's need for cash that I first got involved with the game that was destined to make my fortune. Outside Anhausen and up in the hills lies Augsburg Golf and Country Club. To us Langers it was another world, a place of privilege and wealth where the rich men and women of our area went to play a strange game. As a child I cannot remember ever receiving any pocket money for the simple reason that my parents never seemed to have any to spare. Because of this my elder brother Erwin – he is five years older than me – and my sister Maria – she is three years older – began to caddy occasionally up at the country club. By the time I was eight and a half years old I began pestering my parents to allow Erwin or Maria to take me also to the golf club so that I could earn some money as well.

I was awfully young, of course, but my father realized
I think that it is not easy for an eight-year-old boy to
have to always walk past the sweetshop without being
able to pop inside and buy something, so he agreed to me
offering my inadequate services as a caddy at the club
and, anyway, my brother would be there to show me the
ropes.

So after several lengthy and fairly incomprehensible
lectures from Erwin on the way to caddy properly I was
ready for my inauguration into the mysteries of pulling
a trolley of clubs around a course for someone so rich
they could afford to pay me real money. I recall clearly
that first day when I set off for Augsburg, a five-mile
trip that I covered in near record time on my bicycle, so
eager was I to start my new and lucrative professional
life. By the time I arrived I was dripping with sweat
despite the crispness of the spring morning in the hills.
The system for employment was simple enough.
Having been authenticated by my brother as a person of
deep knowledge about the game and its decorum, I had
to hang around the caddy shed until a member turned
up in need of a caddy. On my very first day I had one of
those lucky breaks which seem irrelevant at the time
but which in retrospect have a deep impact on a whole
life because my first customer was a young man in his
twenties called Manfred Seidel.

The real luck was that Manfred was then the club
champion, a golfer who played off a handicap of three.
And at Augsburg that was good enough to make him
seem like a combination of Nicklaus and Player with a
little Palmer thrown in as well. In truth, Manfred must
have taken some pity on this scrawny, little kid who
was so eager to pull his clubs along on a trolley. I was
always small for my age so I suppose I must have
intrigued him. Whatever the reason, it was a huge
stroke of luck because not only was Manfred the best

player at Augsburg but he was one of the nicest people there as well and we took to each other straight away.

He was very patient with me on that first day, sensing correctly that I was eager to please and that my mistakes were based on ignorance and not petulance. He explained what I should do to become a decent caddy as we played a round and, of course, as a good player I, for my part, was able to see how the game should be played and not have to spend most of my time searching for a ball hacked into the rough by someone who would never be able to hit a golfball with even a degree of efficiency and ability.

At the end of this first round came the best bit as Manfred handed over two marks 50 pfennigs and, after bowing almost to the ground in appreciation, I hurtled back to Anhausen to show my parents what an instant success their youngest son had become that day. I can honestly say that I can still close my eyes and feel the smoothness of those coins as I held them in one hand all the way home and that no cheque, no matter how large, I have received since has given me such a thrill as this first modest pay-packet. Even better news was that Manfred wanted me to caddy for him again.

So suddenly the days began to revolve around golf. The extra money was useful not just for me and my beloved sweetshop but I was also able to contribute to the general household budget and my hard-pressed parents welcomed this fact warmly. During weekdays I would go to school from eight in the morning until noon and then point my bicycle towards Augsburg and munch on a sandwich and an apple as I made the trip to my workplace.

My enthusiasm for work as a caddy at the club was twofold. Firstly, I knew I had only a limited opportunity to make money because the golf season in Germany is restricted to spring and summer as even the most devoted of golfers cannot play the game in freezing conditions and certainly not through the snow of a German winter. Secondly, I had become entranced by the game almost immediately. Sport had always been a love of my life and I was pretty good at almost every game I came across. Although soccer was my top pursuit, as with every young German, this funny game of golf with its mysterious ways intrigued me and presented a challenge I longed to take up.

Unfortunately, I could not present myself to such a challenge immediately. Club rules regarding caddies were very strict and very specific. None of us was allowed to actually play on the course until we had a game warranting a handicap of at least 36. It was the usual Catch-22 situation. I couldn't play unless I had a handicap but how could I get a handicap when I couldn't play?

The answer to this riddle at Augsburg was the same answer so many other caddies have come up with at golf clubs all over the world. We played where we could with what we could and when we could. Over the years a motley collection of clubs had been assembled in the caddy shack. Some had been given by members who took pity on some keen, young caddy and others had been rescued from being hurled on to the local rubbish dump. There were not many clubs and the ones we had were not exactly finely honed instruments.

I seem to recall that I had access to a two wood and a three iron, a seven iron and a putter. Each club had a bamboo shaft that was so whippy you were in danger of breaking your wrists if you took it back too far or too quickly. At first I just watched the older caddies play but soon I became bored by this and, indeed, throughout my life I have never been a good spectator of any game, always itching instead to participate.

So when possible I borrowed a club and went off to the

driving range where we were allowed to practise as long as we were not upsetting any of the members. This was usually not a problem for the course was quiet by day, especially in the early part of the week. I spent hours hitting balls on that practice ground, discovering what I could and could not do and why the ball went left or right or even – sometimes – straight.

When I wasn't on the practice ground I would work around the putting green. I never had a pitching wedge or a sand wedge so I had to learn how to improvise with a seven iron. In retrospect, it was the best way to learn. There were a lot of mistakes but I learned how to try to control the ball in various ways. It taught me the art of shot-making, of improvisation and of using my imagination to create a shot that would get the ball reasonably close to the hole. It is the same way that great stars like Severiano Ballesteros and Lee Trevino learned the game and it is, I believe, the best because in later life it offers so many extra options to a player when confronted with an unexpected problem in a major event.

Back then, however, such future problems were not my concern. My main worry was finding enough time in the day to earn much-needed cash as a caddy and to indulge my passion for the game itself. It was a problem I overcame by moving out of my home and moving into the club itself for the summer holidays. Along with a few close friends we used to take our tents up there and pitch them in the woods during the good weather. It meant we wasted no time travelling the not inconsiderable distance from home and besides that it was good fun.

Although I was still small I was exceptionally strong for a nine year old. All my cycling and my bag carrying had built up my strength better than if I had embarked on a weight-lifting course. Back then my energy seemed limitless. I wish it was the same today. Certainly by the time I was ten years old I was able to play at least 36 holes a day – and sometimes more – plus I would caddy as well. Often in order to earn more money I would carry one set of clubs and pull a second set on a cart. It was quite a sight and one that caused much amusement to many members to see this little guy working so hard.

I didn't mind the smiles because I felt they respected me and what I was trying to do. Certainly I was a fairly popular caddy, earning myself the nickname 'Adlerauge' which means 'Eagle-eye' because I always kept my eye on the ball and prided myself on the fact that none of my customers ever lost a ball in the rough. But I am shooting ahead of myself and how I came to actually get out on the golf course to play golf.

The professional at the club when I started caddying at eight was a man called Sooky Maharaj who was of Indian descent but actually came from Trinidad. Maharaj, despite having the sunny, outgoing disposition of most Trinidadians, remained as far as caddies were concerned a remote figure. To me at any rate he seemed quite fearsome. After several weeks spent practising until my hands felt as though they belonged to someone else, I determined to ask this pro if I was adroit enough to attack the course as a player.

I recall how I began to walk up to Sooky several times but turned away at the last moment before speaking to him. I was scared in case he rejected me straight away. Eventually, one of my friends said that if I didn't go to ask then he would do it on my behalf. Well, I've always had this strong desire to make my own mistakes and to carve out my own destiny so I finally asked if he would test me to see if I was competent enough to play.

Sooky told me to turn up early the next morning and report to him on the practice ground where he would check me out. It was the signal for a sleepless night, an evening spent chewing at my fingernails and a desperate last practice session to perfect what must have been no more than a partially controlled lunge at the ball. Next day I reported to the great man.

Until then the professional had been only a distant figure to me, as to the other caddies. If he saw us practising he might glance at us briefly but he never, ever offered either words of encouragement or advice. I don't know why. Our closest contact came when he got one of us to pick up his own practice balls on the driving range for which he paid us a few pfennigs. To be fair to him, however, he treated my test with the seriousness I myself brought to the occasion and when I had hit about ten balls he merely said I looked as though I wouldn't chew up the course too much and that I could play when the proper opportunity presented itself.

I was overjoyed. It was now July, just three and a half months on from the first day I had cycled to the club to work as a caddy and here I was a competent golfer. Or so it seemed. Even now I am proud of that achievement. I have no idea whether I appeared impressive to Maharaj or to anyone else but I recall that I at least found little difficulty in actually striking the ball and that I was confident of giving it a clout every time I swung the club. I knew also from my time spent caddying for the club champion that the secret of success at golf was not so much in how far you hit the ball but where it ended up. Even by the end of that first summer I had caddied for enough hackers to realize that time spent searching in the rough was time wasted. I cannot claim, unfortunately, to have followed this piece of intuitive wisdom ever since. But I have tried.

3

A pro at last

As Bernhard grew up apparently thriving on his hectic diet of school, football, golf and work as a caddy, so too did his reputation grow at the Augsburg Golf and Country Club. The little boy who had so amused and intrigued the members as a hard-working eight year old had matured into a teenager of some detectable ability as far as golf was concerned. Even more impressive was his commitment to becoming the best player his potential allowed. Work comes naturally to him. His success ultimately at the game can be attributed, I believe, as much to his single-minded determination and his belief in himself as it can to a naturally fluent technique. Even so, as the time approached when the Langer family had to debate job options for the youngest son, golf was not top of the list. Indeed as far as his parents were concerned initially it was not even on the list at all.

Back in the late sixties golf was hardly a going concern in West Germany. The game was still the exclusive plaything of the wealthy and for the Langer family the weekly search for enough money to keep body, soul and stomach in reasonable shape remained an urgent one. Certainly the idea that Bernhard could make his way in the world via this preposterous game seemed out of the question. Yet when the time came for Bernhard to leave school it was golf that claimed him. This is not only a tribute to his own determination to carve out a living within the sport but to his parents' desire to see their son happy as well as earning money. When I spoke with him about this formative period of his life, Bernhard and I were sitting in one of the lavish reception rooms at Woburn Abbey where he was a guest of the Marquis of Tavistock while he played in the Dunhill Masters. The backdrop to our conversation was stunning and as we chatted Bernhard could not help but smile as he contrasted this opulent room with another modest little building that was once the very epicentre of his sporting universe...

When we were not caddying, playing or practising at Augsburg we usually spent our time in the caddy-shack. Here we had a football machine that regularly witnessed re-runs of various World Cups. It was here that we used to discuss which members were good to caddy for, which were terrible and which tipped the most. I remember there was a married couple whom nobody liked to work for. It was not that they were miserly – usually they paid very well – but an afternoon spent with them was like a few hours in a battle zone.

Neither he nor she could play the game really but they took it very, very seriously and both had an awful temper. Even before leaving the first tee they would be arguing and fighting and the atmosphere was always really bad. Most of the caddies hid when they saw their car draw up but because I needed the money I used to volunteer for the job. Eventually, even I had had enough of this tiresome duo and often they had to pull their own clubs around because, mysteriously, all the caddies seemed to disappear at once.

By now I was 14 and approaching the end of my school life. My six years at the golf club had taught me much about the game and a fair bit about life itself and the complexities of the human personality. However, I had still not had a formal golf lesson. I had learned to play the game by watching the better players and copying them and by sheer relentless practice, learning from my own mistakes along the way. Indeed not only had I not had a lesson but I had never even read a book on how the game should be played. The nearest I came to doing that was gazing at Jack Nicklaus's swing sequence, a faded eight-frame article some caddy had torn out of a magazine and stuck on the caddy-shack wall years earlier.

Every move of that sequence, even the colour of Nicklaus's sweater and trousers, is stamped indelibly on my memory. The Holy Grail itself cannot have been gazed at with more reverence or concentration than I afforded this sequence. I would then spend hours out on the driving range checking my own hand and arm alignment and imagining I was swinging the club exactly like the great man himself. Anyone who knows my swing today will realize how much this teenager was deluding himself.

Whatever type of swing I had, however, it was reasonably effective at getting the ball round Augsburg in decent scores. If I had been a member of the club then I would have been one of the best players; as it was I could lay claim to being one of the best caddies. The highpoint of my year at this time came deep into autumn when the club staged the annual caddy championship. For years I had done well, finishing in the top three several times but never actually winning. Now at 14 years old I gave it one last great effort and went round in 73 only to be beaten by a guy who stood two heads taller than me and who always seemed to go round in one or two strokes better than me. It was a bitter disappointment at the time but one I have learned to live with, consoling myself with the thought that this same caddy is now a pro himself and rarely manages to beat 80. Maybe we should have another match together at Augsburg.

I was also supplementing my caddy earnings by giving some members strictly unofficial lessons. They asked me for these lessons on the course during the round and I was flattered to hand on what I had learned myself as they played, as well as grateful for the extra money. The professional would not have been too happy if he had known what was happening. Admittedly, it was all pretty basic stuff but then so many of the members just did not have a clue about how to grip the club correctly, how to stand to the ball, how to aim at the target and how to actually swing the club at the ball, rather than merely launch themselves in a manner that threatened terminal damage to their spines.

So I suppose I was a professional before even I realized what being a pro entailed. Because I never had the money to join a club I can never claim to have been an amateur anyway. It is something I regret very much. Knowing now what a wide world amateur golf encompasses and the opportunities it presents not only for playing the game around the world but in the area of education as well I wish I had had the chance of playing as an amateur. Back then, however, such a desirable world was way beyond my position in life as well as my pocket.

For some time I had divided my sporting life between football and golf. I was good at both and I saw no reason why I should not indulge my love for both sports more or less equally. As a footballer I was lucky enough to play for Anhausen, a selection that was worth a lot of kudos in the town's teenage society. Although still small for my age I liked to play centre forward and delighted in beating much larger defenders with speed and agility. Of course, sometimes these same large defenders delighted in battering me to the ground. For some reason, however, my mother decided that I had to choose between football and golf.

The big football matches – big for me anyway – were always on a Saturday or a Sunday, which coincided with the busiest period at the golf club and the two days in which I could earn most money as a caddy. I think my mother was worried that I was taking too much out of myself by playing soccer and then haring off to Augsburg to carry golf clubs round for the rest of the day. All mothers, I suppose, are the same over these things. Anyway for a time I pretended that I was concentrating on football before sneaking off to Augsburg but gradually I discovered that I was spending more time at golf, that I was more interested in it as a game and although I continued playing soccer until I was 20 football from that point on was secondary.

Around the same time I had to think seriously about what I wanted to try to do when I left school. All I knew for certain was that I wanted to be involved in golf. As I would never have the sort of job that would have earned me enough money to have actually joined a club, I automatically assumed that my future in golf was as a

professional. It was an audacious decision for me to
make at 14, with my background, but at the time it made
logical and sound sense. If I had suggested such a thing
to my parents even a year or so earlier they would have
laughed but when I told them what my plans were they
agreed to help me in whatever way they could.

Their decision to indulge me in my passion for the
game was helped by the fact that I had proved in this
last schoolboy summer that there was significant
money to be made from the sport. I had bought for
myself with money earned at Augsburg a wonderful
racing bicycle that had cost 250 marks. This repre-
sented a small fortune to the Langer family and my
parents were duly impressed.

There was still some opposition to overcome, however, before I took my first tentative step towards my
present career and lifestyle. One of the members I
caddied for regularly went to Munich for lessons from a
professional called Heinz Fehring. It was from this
member that I learned one day that the club in Munich
was looking for a new assistant professional.

So I contacted Herr Fehring and told him that I
wanted to apply for the job and that members at the
Augsburg Club would vouch for my enthusiasm and my
competence. Heinz's reply did not hand me the post on a
plate but it was reassuring. If I was really serious then
they would speak to me.

First though I had to get my parents' permission and
although they were keen for me to do what I wanted
they still had some reservations about my plunging
headlong into golf. As a school-leaver I was obliged to
talk with the Careers Adviser at the local Job Centre. He
asked me what I wanted to do and I replied I wished to
become a golf pro. 'What,' he asked, 'is a golf pro?' He
went on to tell me that such a job was not a profession,
that it was not an 'official job' and that, as it was not

approved by the government, that he could not recommend I follow my dream. Instead he advised me to go off and learn a proper job before indulging my youthful and idiotic ambition. My parents, understandably, agreed with him; I didn't.

Somehow I persuaded my parents to come with me to Munich to meet the club president and Heinz and to see what being an assistant pro entailed. It was the biggest day of my life and, thankfully, it went well. The Munich people impressed my parents with their sincerity and at last my parents agreed that if they wanted me to work there then I could go. It was a tough decision for my mother because Munich was one and a half hours away by car, too far to commute, and it meant she was losing her 'baby' in dramatic fashion. She was only truly satisfied when the club found a farmhouse with a room for me and a family to look after me and when she saw there was a Catholic Church near enough for me to attend each Sunday. Religion then, as now, was very important not only to my mother but to me also.

So I signed a contract with the Munich Club for three and a half years. It was worth 300 marks a month; it stated that I would apply myself diligently to all aspects of learning how to become a proficient professional and that the club in return would afford me the appropriate facilities and opportunities to absorb my new trade. I was one month short of my 15th birthday when I went to Munich. I was young, I was apprehensive, but I was excited. My new life had begun.

Initially it was a very lonely life. I managed to go home every six weeks or so for a couple of days and how I longed for those weekends back in the comforting familiarity of Anhausen. I missed my family and my friends and more than one night I lay awake wondering what on earth I was doing in this strange, far-off place. It is a feeling that still comes back to me today when I am lying in another hotel room on the other side of the world after a bad day out on the course.

Nowadays, of course, I can use jets to take me home swiftly even if occasionally my clubs fail to make it back with me; but back then in Munich as a 15-year-old boy all I had was a bicycle and with Munich itself half an hour's car ride away, I was effectively trapped. The only people I had contact with were the members, the secretary and the four or five pros at this fashionable club. It was hardly the sort of company any self-respecting teenager would seek out. But I was stuck with it and as the days turned into weeks my life once more took on a reassuring routine.

Part of my training meant going to business school. There was no specific course for what I was trying to learn – golf, after all, was not officially approved – so I was lumped in with a bunch of trainee salesmen who were being taught how to sell sporting goods. Once a week I was at school from eight in the morning until two in the afternoon. Then I would have to work in the club shop for at least a couple of hours and I also had to fit in lessons in English. At that time part of the final test for any aspiring golf professional in Germany was the ability to communicate in English. I was greatly relieved when one of the lady members offered to coach me in this language which was still strange to me even though I had studied it at school.

It meant that most days were busy but even so the senior professionals always managed to ensure that I had time to go out on the practice ground to hit balls and to play a few holes, if not a full round, regularly. I am often astonished, as well as saddened, to note that in England of all places such little emphasis is placed on allowing aspiring young assistant professionals to actually play the game and give more golf lessons. Too often they seem to be used as mere shop assistants, their

talent and their enthusiasm for the sport gradually
slipping away until, in frustration, they pack it in. It is a
disgraceful state of affairs and one that I hope will
change in the near future.

Being able to play regularly at a course as good as
Munich was terrific for me, however. There were some
very good young amateurs at the club, guys who were
scratch or one handicap and they were always keen to
have a match with me. I had never had a handicap but
by 15 I was probably scratch at best and a two handicap
at worst. We always played these matches off level and
usually I took the members on in the long summer
evenings before cycling back to my small room in the
nearby village. Meanwhile, Heinz Fehring took a great
interest in my game. It was the first time in my life that
a qualified golfer, a pro, had looked closely at what I
was doing. Suddenly I wasn't alone on my voyage of
discovery.

Heinz changed my grip, my address position and
several other things, so that I could begin to actually
'work' the ball and not just whack it. For 18 months he
watched my development as a golfer and as a person,
and worked long hours with me. Then, as I approached
my 17th birthday, he asked me a question that was to
change my life again. He asked me if I wanted to be a
playing pro - or a teaching pro. It was a question I had
debated for many hours with myself. By now I was
aware that there was a big world out there where men
and women made money - and some made a lot of
money - from just playing the game to the best of their
ability. My answer to Heinz was instant - I wanted to be
a playing professional, to earn my money on the
European Tour.

4

The travelling begins..
and so does the heartache

Langer's decision to seek his fortune as a playing professional was an easy one for a young man to make. It was, however, something else to turn his dream into a reality. There was no tradition in Germany for such a thing, no heroic national figure from whom he could draw inspiration. Until Bernhard himself changed everything the fact is that Germany's contribution to world class golf had been on a par with the Seychelles' donation to global literature. Even the European Tour itself in the mid-seventies was still a delicate and sometimes chaotic thing. Since Tony Jacklin had single-handedly revitalized golf in Britain with his victories in the British and US Opens, the Tour had been growing in stature and in prize money but sponsors were still fickle and the Continental section of the Tour was a long way from the strong, money-laden circuit it is today.

For Langer the personal challenge was twofold. First, he had to find enough money to enable him to travel round Europe. Secondly, he had to improve his game and in particular to sharpen his competitive edge. The best way to achieve this, of course, was to learn, once again, the hard way... by making his mistakes and absorbing his lessons on the Tour itself. Heinz Fehring had a good enough eye to realize the young man had a chance and he was determined that this resolute teenager should be given the opportunity to explore fully the outer limits of his ability. As with all the best stories this was the cue for one of those happy coincidences to occur that not only shape a life but change the direction in which a person is travelling. In Langer's case his opportunity arose because Fehring knew a keen golfer called Jan Brugelman, and because Munich got involved in a four-club competition.

After I had told Heinz that I wanted to be a playing pro, he made sure that I had more time to practise. Suddenly I was able to hit hundreds of balls a day instead of dozens and my game improved significantly. It was around this time that I took part in my first really significant competition, involving players from Munich, Frankfurt, Stuttgart and Garmisch-Partenkirchen.

Each club put in a team made up of the best amateurs and the best professionals and we played over two days at Munich. The professionals played for money and when the competition started I was not being mentioned when anyone spoke of the eventual winner from the pros' section. It was hardly surprising for most of the other pros had never even heard of Bernhard Langer. Yet despite being just 16 and very nervous I won the first prize, beating two or three of the country's top professionals to pocket 500 marks. It got me some publicity which was nice – but I was more impressed with the money!

It seemed to me quite extraordinary that I could earn in two days what it took me two months to make as an assistant professional. Now, more than ever, I thought that this was the life for me. As my confidence grew, I entered other tournaments with Heinz always encouraging me to have a go and making sure I had the time to practise before these events. My big breakthrough came in 1975 when, just 17, I won the German National Open after beating off the challenge of two other players in a play-off that took place at Cologne despite a monumental thunderstorm.

Jan Brugelman was watching that day. Nowadays Jan is president of the German Golf Federation but then he was just a golf fanatic. When Heinz mentioned to him that I was looking for a sponsor to go on the European Tour, Jan advised that I should contact him nearer the time I was actually going to make the move. The next year I did just that and Jan told me to come to see him in Cologne.

When we met, Jan offered me a deal. He would pay me a regular monthly wage and in return I would give him 50 per cent of any prize money. It meant that I always knew I had enough money to feed myself and to find a roof over my head if I was careful and I did not hesitate before shaking hands with my benefactor. When I left Jan to travel back to Munich, I was elated. I was also scared. I had come a long way since leaving Anhausen but despite being a national champion I was still just a kid and I wasn't sure what I was going to find out there in the world or if I was big enough to handle it.

Like it or not, however, I was now firmly embarked on a course of action from which I could not flinch. Too many people had shown belief in me for me to let them down and anyway I desperately wanted to find out for myself if I had what it takes.

Winning the National Open – restricted to German-born golfers – had earned me 6000 marks. With the money I bought my first car, a Ford Escort. The car was bright yellow and I polished it until my arms ached. Then in early February 1976 I packed my suitcase, put my clubs into the boot and set off for the Mediterranean coast. My first tournament was to be the Portuguese Open but I had decided to stop off en route to practise on some of the courses around Marbella. I was quite rusty after the usual German winter and I needed to work on my swing. Anyway the sun would do me good and I wanted to look the part when I pitched up at Quinta do Lago in Portugal.

Because my financial resources were limited, I could not afford to waste any time on this trip. So I left my departure until the last possible moment and then travelled the 1600 mile journey to Marbella in one go. It took me 25 hours solid driving and I felt I had been drugged with something by the time I pulled into Marbella. All I wanted to do was to sleep. First though I had to find a hotel. To be honest the word 'hotel' is an outrageously inaccurate description of where I ended up. I simply dared not afford the prices asked by proper hotels and so I ended up in a very basic place. Just four walls and a washbasin. It was no more than a doss-house, the sort of place I would not send my dog to today.

There were bugs crawling everywhere, including the bed. It was so bad that I kept the light on all night because if I turned it off I could hear things moving under the bed or somewhere in the room and I didn't feel too happy about that. When I woke up in the morning, I was covered in bites. I had never felt so alone. Soon enough I got used to these doss-houses all over Europe, even grading them according to my own 'star' system so that if anyone wants to know the cheapest places to stay on holiday I can tell them straight away. I think I could arrange a package deal for someone to travel all over Europe on very little money. The only problem is that after staying in these places you would need a month in hospital to recover.

It is funny now to look back on but at the time it was anything but a laugh. People who moan about sportsmen being too pampered these days should realize that this is how many of us started. And still start. I don't regret it either because it has given me a genuine perspective on life and, especially, on money. I spent as little time as possible in these awful places, working on my game all day and every day, dreading the time when I must return to some dingy little room with its scruffy sheets and the smell of a recent occupant still hanging in the air.

But like most young people I survived my ordeal and when I turned up at the Portuguese Open that year on the Algarve I tried to look as though I'd stepped out of a five-star hotel and not a dump. I may have succeeded in that deception but I did not succeed in the tournament itself, missing the second cut on Saturday by several shots. So it was back to Spain and the Spanish Open, held that year further up the coast from Marbella at La Manga. There it was the same story. Lousy digs and an early exit from big-time golf after two rounds. I was finding out the hard way that being good in Germany meant not a lot on the European Tour.

I pointed my by now not-so-bright yellow Escort inland and headed for the Madrid Open. Staged as

always at the Puerta de Hierro club in the ritzy suburbs
of that great city, the Madrid Open is a terrific
tournament with a rich history. The club is very grand
with polo grounds and many wealthy members as well
as aristocrats, including the King of Spain himself. I
was impressed with it all but especially with the course
which is hilly, demanding, difficult and a true test. I
liked it straight away.

The course requires long and straight hitting off the
tee and accurate approach play. I thrived on this
challenge and played well. I made the cut and finished
fifth in my third tournament on the European scene.
Eddie Polland won the title and although the media
attention was understandably focused on the wise-
cracking Irishman I got quite a few mentions in
newspapers and magazines as a name to watch for in
the future. I was thrilled, naturally. My gamble had
begun to pay off and I was now on my way to a true
golfing career. Suddenly my horizons changed, my
ambition grew and my expectations soared as well. It
was at this time that my putting went crazy.

Up to this time I had never been a great putter but I
had certainly been a good one. Now, although I was still
competent at long putting, I began to lose control of my
putter as soon as I got close to the hole. It was awful.
Terrible. A year earlier I had had my first taste of panic
as far as playing golf is concerned. It came after I had
agreed to play a match against two fairly high-
handicap but wealthy members at Munich. The stakes
were high – for me anyway. So much so that I turned up
early that day to hit 50 practice balls. My first swing on
that practice ground sent a ball scuttering away at right
angles. I had shanked, something I had hardly ever
done before in my life. The second ball did the same.
And the third. I swear, though it is hard to believe, that I
shanked every one of those 50 balls so that by the time I

got to the tee I was almost a gibbering wreck.

Under the pretence that I wasn't feeling too well – not that dishonest a claim actually – I suggested we reduce the stakes. Reluctantly my partners agreed and we played a 10-mark Nassau. I drove off expecting the worst. Instead the ball flew beautifully off the middle of my driver and screamed down the fairway. I ended up shooting 69 that day, won about 80 marks and finished the round delighted but bewildered. The lesson here, I thought, is that you never know what is going to happen in this game or how you are going to play. As a general rule this is true enough but now as I struggled on the greens for several weeks after my triumph at Madrid I realized that there was another golfing rule to be absorbed which is that just when you think things are about as bad as they can be, they tend to get worse.

Now things got very bad indeed. Heinz changed my putting grip, but it made little difference. I had set out to make a reputation for myself on the Tour and I was succeeding in the wrong way. People were coming out to watch me play but it was in the manner of those people who go to car races hoping to see a crash. Every time I got anywhere from two feet to six feet from the hole an expectant hush would fall on the gallery. Not the sporting silence that allows a golfer to hit his ball in peace but the sort that makes you look up expecting to see vultures circling even though you cannot hear their wings beating. They had come to see this youngster who could get the ball close to the hole but then struggled to get the thing in.

I rarely let them down. To the spectators it must have seemed like watching a man suffer a very public nervous breakdown as I stood over my ball, muscles tensing, colour draining from my face. I finally reached breaking point in 1977 when I defended my German Open title and averaged 40 putts per round. It was a form of sporting suicide. In the first round at the second hole I knocked my approach shot into six feet. I hit my first putt so fast that I double-hit the ball and despite striking the back of the hole it still went past by 10 inches. From there it took me two more putts to get down. Four putts from six feet! If I didn't know it before I now knew that I was really in trouble.

Sympathy poured over me from all sides but, though it was nice that people and especially fellow professionals should care, my putting stroke over those short putts still remained a terrible sight. The more I missed, the worse I got. It got so I was expecting to miss. Frequently I would be completely frozen over the ball. My brain just would not instruct my body to carry out the necessary action because the usual result was heartbreaking. I felt as though I had no control over my arms and hands at all. It was as though they belonged to someone else and this other person hated me. I had no backswing, executing instead a blurred jab with the putter that was so quick many people missed it altogether.

I played in my first Hennessey Cup that year and my putting was so bad that I wasn't allowed to play until the Saturday and Sunday of the competition because everyone knew how I was suffering on the greens. Fortunately, I did not realize then that the problem was to stay with me for years, rather than months. Even so I did consider quitting. I knew my ball-stroking was good enough to make the top 10 in Europe, that all I had to do was to improve my putting average so I gave myself three years' maximum to do just that. If the putting failed to improve then I was going to find something else to do with my life. The alternative – of stuttering around Europe for years – was too awful to contemplate and certainly too draining in reality to put up with for years.

Meanwhile I knew I was a good enough player to pick up a cheque here and there and, as I was not expecting to become a millionaire, I decided to continue as best I could. It was, however, hard. I was frustrated by my putting problems and at times the whole thing got me down completely. I read articles pointing out that I was very young to be suffering the 'yips', the golfer's name for this strange disease that strikes out of a clear blue sky and which has caused so many fine careers to end prematurely. But, contrary to popular thinking, I did not delve into the subject myself. I was afraid to do that because I felt that if I understood the mechanics of the problem too much that I would never get rid of the affliction. Silly maybe, but that is how I felt.

Some commentators remain convinced that I underwent hypnosis, that I tried out some weird 'witch doctor' cures or that ultimately I entered into a pact with the devil. Good copy for the journalists but none of these stories is true. I just did what I've always done in my life when something has gone wrong... I worked harder than ever before. The problem was that every time I played, my fellow professionals would give me advice. I would then rush off to the practice putting green to put these new ideas into action and there several more pros would give me different and conflicting advice. I must have spent thousands of hours on putting greens and talked to hundreds of other golfers but in the end I cured myself by sheer hard graft.

There was no miracle cure, no sudden inspiration. Instead my problem was cured because I was determined that I would overcome it. It was a case of mind over matter and a tremendous amount of practice. It worked. My putting improved to the point where I was at least an average player on the greens and though that was not good enough to win tournaments it was adequate and meant that my weekly pay cheques from the tour improved. In 1976 I had won £2129 and finished 90th on the money list. In 1977, with my putting at its worst and playing fewer events because I was also doing my National Service in the German Air Force, I made only £690 and did not even figure in the rankings. But in 1978 I was 40th with £7706 to my name and the following year I earned almost £8000 on the tour.

Then in 1979 I won the Cacharel Under-25 Championship in Nîmes, France, by a record 17 shots. It was a terrific boost to my career and to my confidence. Even when I hit a bad putt in that event it seemed to go into the hole. After all the problems I had suffered it seemed as though someone had at last decided to smile at me. I simply could not stop laughing.

5

Real success… and more heartache

Victory in the Cacharel Under-25 Championship in 1979 was worth £2780 to Langer. It brought his total winnings for the year to £7972 and 25 pence. In the Order of Merit – as the money list was still quaintly called in those days – Langer finished the season in 56th position. Although he finished the year with a flourish when he won the South American Order of Merit, playing in five events and finishing in the top five each time to pick up a 10,000 dollar bonus, it meant that in some ways 1979 had been a disappointment for the hungry young man.

Twelve months previously he had finished 40th in Europe and had done so with a better stroke average than in 1979 (73.73 compared to 74.15) so that there were those who began to feel that the first German with potential to hit the tour was not going to be anything other than a bread and butter golfer. Yet there was another statistic that was overlooked at the time but which suggested quite the opposite. In 1978 Langer had played in 16 Tour events and missed the cut in six of them, whereas in 1979 he again played 16 tournaments but this time he missed only two halfway cuts. It was a significant advance. It meant that the fledgling pro was achieving the sort of consistency that wins money and eventually wins titles. It meant Langer was learning not just how to play golf properly but how to be a professional. When this fact is coupled to his heroic performance in the Cacharel event and his dramatically improved putting average, then the evidence was there for all but a superficial observer to acknowledge that here was a player of genuine quality.

As 1980 dawned, Langer felt more confident than ever before. He felt he had served his apprenticeship and that the time had come for another great step forward. It was a view shared by many of his peers. The way he had adjusted to the demands of a touring golfer's life, his commitment, his passion for practice and his determination to succeed had impressed many by the end of 1979. It is an indisputable fact that young golfers of true quality appear regularly on the European scene but too often many of them allow the rewards of relative success to deflect them from something more distant and harder to attain. In other words they achieve a little too quickly and then rest on their laurels for a couple of years before disappearing from the scene. Hard work and persistent graft is not everyone's idea of fun especially in a game where the physical demands are not high but where the physical pleasures available are second to none. Langer, however, was never tempted from the straight and narrow. Despite this, he was to be tried sorely once more, for just as he seemed about to blossom as a golfer, his putting went as crazy as ever.

Once you have suffered putting problems you know as a golfer that it can happen again. I did not know why I'd had trouble in the first place so how on earth could I really believe that there would never be another setback? It was not, however, a subject that consumed me. By 1980 I was happy with my game and my form. I knew for sure that I could make a living from golf and that, after all, was all I'd ever really wanted. Of course as I grew older, a little wiser and a lot more mature I began to appreciate just how rich the pickings were in this game. It called for sacrifice but to a poor boy like I had once been this sacrifice never seemed very much at all.

My goal for 1980 was simple to set but considerably more difficult to achieve. I wanted to finish the year in the top 10 in the money list. By the middle of the summer it seemed more reasonable to hope for a top 40 place and even then that was not assured. I was still playing well enough and my putting had not gone haywire but the fact remained that on the greens I was just not getting enough birdie putts in to challenge.

The change in fortunes, when it came, did not come about because I executed some precise and clever plan but because of a couple of chance occurrences. The first of these came during the Hennessey Cup match at Sunningdale, that fabulous course a few miles down the road from Wentworth. It was while I was on the practice putting green there that Seve Ballesteros came over and asked if he could have a look at my putter.

Seve has never been a guy who disguises his opinion

on anything and he was swift and to the point when he held my club and inspected it carefully. 'No wonder you are not putting very well. This putter is awful. Far too light. No one could putt well with this thing,' he said before striding back to his own practice session.

From the putting green to the pro shop at Sunningdale is a distance of no more than 30 yards, so within seconds of my conversation with Seve I was in the shop and explaining my predicament to Clive Clark. Clive, now one of the main BBC Television commentators, was the pro at Sunningdale in those days and he advised me to go and have a look in his barrel of clubs because there was a selection of putters there that had been traded in and I just might find something I could work on.

I had a look at several putters and then came across an old Bullseye model that had once belonged to an equally old lady. She had given up on it but the moment I took the club in my hands I knew it was the right one for me. It just felt right, sort of comfortable. I asked Clive how much he wanted for it and we settled on five pounds. It was one of the better investments of my life.

The following week I had my best finish to date in a Tour event when I came second in the Tournament Players' Championship. The week after that I finished third in the Bob Hope Classic. Seven days later I was a winner at last.

Victory came at the Dunlop Masters which was held just inside Wales at the St Pierre Club near Chepstow. It was a glorious week with the sun shining on everyone and on me in particular. I had never felt so good before in my life. With my new putter I felt I could take on the world. Even so, few people noticed me too much before the tournament began. Most of the Press interest centred on the duel taking place between Sandy Lyle and Greg Norman for the number one spot on the

European Tour. As far as the journalists were concerned I was just another bit player that week. It seemed they were right when America's Hubert Green opened up with a 67 to lead after day one. Then Green struggled to a 77; I followed up my opening 70 with a 65 to find myself in the lead and never looked back.

I had often wondered how I would react when I found myself in the right position to actually win. That week at Chepstow I discovered the truth – I loved being in the lead and I enjoyed winning more than anything else. I shot 67 on the third day and ended with a 68 for a record 14 under par total of 270 to win by five strokes from Brian Barnes. When I came to the last hole, a tricky 200 yard-plus par three I had so many shots in hand that I was more relaxed than I had been at the halfway point. My ordeal had turned into a victory waltz and I was elated. Just for the record, Lyle finished fifth to head Norman for the top money spot that year.

No one, however, finished that year better than me. Having gone second, third, fifth, first, I then added a third place in the Lancôme Invitational in Paris to take my winnings from four tournaments to over £20,000, my total for the year to almost £33,000 and to clinch ninth place in the Money List. I had achieved my early goal of a top 10 spot. As somebody has said, if you aim for the stars then you just might hit the moon. That winter back in Germany I was very definitely over the moon with my performance.

So too, naturally, were my parents. At last I had shown that I really could earn a very good living from golf and in my village of Anhausen at least my fame had spread. It was a very happy time for me but I knew that I wanted more. It is the feeling that comes with triumph that is the true reward and I was now addicted to this drug and this life.

So after only a few days away from golf I began

working on my game again with my coach, Willi
Hoffman. I had first met Willi in the early seventies
through Heinz Fehring and gradually over the years I
had become dependent on him when I had a problem. As
I'm not a supremely natural golfer my swing was
constantly in need of some fine tuning. I still see Willi
several times a year for an overhaul and he is now not
only my coach but one of my very best friends.

Our relationship is so close, we know each other so
well and, more important, he knows my swing so well
that he can spot in seconds what needs adjusting. I trust
him implicitly for I know he will not try to con me in any
way. Like every other golfer it is the same errors that
constantly creep into my game and Willi knows all my
weak points. I always consult him before any important
event no matter how I feel I am playing and we speak
often on the telephone wherever I am in the world.

In the winter of 1980–81 I worked very hard with Willi
to improve my game for the following season. I had
made one breakthrough but now I was determined to
make another one. I wanted to be number one in Europe.
Sometimes I got depressed as I failed to perfect some
slight improvement in my game, and my mother would
worry. She would try to tell me that it did not matter if I
did not win, that the important thing was to be healthy
and not to drive myself too hard. Like most mothers, she
was right but she could not stop me pushing on towards
some distant goal that only I could see.

I wanted to prove to everyone that my form at the end
of 1980 was not a fluke and that I could do even better.
When, eventually, it was time for the new European
season to start I came out of Anhausen like a supremely
trained athlete. I carried with me that year as I left
home the sort of confidence that only comes when a
person knows that he could not have worked harder. I
simply could not wait to get started. The first tourna-

ment in Europe that year was the Madrid Open and I finished fourth. The following week in the Italian Open I was third. Then in the French Open I took second place.

Then it was off to England for the Martini International at Wentworth where mathematical logic seemed to suggest that I would win. Unfortunately, two plus two does not always equal four in life and I finished second again. Still, although frustrated at not winning despite getting myself into position every week, I was happy enough as I was top of the Money List and my reputation was growing almost daily. My rise towards the top in 1981 coincided with a bad year for Seve Ballesteros.

After winning the Open in 1979 and the US Masters in 1980, Seve was the biggest young star in the game. In 1981, however, he seemed to have some trouble coming to terms with what had happened to him. He had a series of highly publicized rows with sponsors over appearance money and for the first time in his meteoric career the Press began to criticize him. Whether he was right or wrong does not matter. The fact remains, however, that as Seve suffered, I prospered and the world's golf writers were happy to write about a new name. Mine.

When I finished second in the Open to Bill Rogers at Sandwich that year I picked up my biggest ever cheque, £17,500, and virtually guaranteed myself the top spot in Europe that season. It was the first of several close finishes in the Open that I have had in the eighties but it was the one that made me realize that I had what it takes to win a major title. In total I played 18 European events in 1981 - including the World Matchplay - and did not miss a single halfway cut.

I won two titles, the German Open and the Bob Hope Classic, and finished second on seven occasions. My total winnings in Europe came to £95,990 which topped the Money List and my stroke average was 70.56, almost two strokes per round better than the previous year. I had also had my first taste of the United States when I was invited to the World Series. I almost won that too, leading with six holes to play but although I failed in that bid my confidence was boosted yet again.

I also took part in my first Ryder Cup when I joined the other Europeans at Walton Heath to compete against probably the strongest side ever assembled by the Americans. Predictably, we were thrashed but I enjoyed myself hugely, halving my own singles against Bruce Lietzke and winning two points over the three days. The Ryder Cup that year had brought with it more than its fair share of controversy but I shall return to this subject later.

It had been a watershed year for me. Five seasons after my first tentative steps outside Germany I was the top money earner on the tour. I had won often enough to show that I possessed whatever is required. I was elated. There was nowhere to go except on to further success and my ambition knew no boundaries.

Yet within a few months of the 1982 season I was plunged back into the depths of near-despair when my putting suddenly disintegrated once again. As before my short-putting went haywire. I was still playing well and earning money but I really started to worry when I partnered Greg Norman in a Men v Women match at Woburn which was staged for television. My putting that week was so awful it was embarrassing. Poor Greg, a much more sensitive man than many suspect, tried his best to gee me up but even his Australian good humour failed to lift me. I finished that week knowing that I must do something to improve my putting or I would go mad.

Before when I had struggled on the greens I had

consoled myself with the thought that, at worst, I could earn a living from golf but since then I had tasted significant success and the prospect of having a potentially terrific career taken from my grasp at this late stage was almost too awful to contemplate.

At least this time it wasn't the 'yips'. The truth is that I have not yipped since 1980. My problem in 1982 was that I was decelerating almost every time I tried to hit the ball. It was an almost Pavlovian response to the challenge of putting the ball. Part of my brain just seized up. I decided that if my brain would not do as I commanded it to do then I must somehow trick it. The outward problem was my hands.

So I came up with the idea of changing my grip. I started putting with my left hand below my right and although it felt very strange to start with I immediately began making a much better stroke, of actually getting the clubhead through the ball and on line with the target. After about three months and many, many hours of practice this 'back-handed' grip began to feel natural.

By the end of the season I was putting better than ever and I have never suffered as badly on the greens ever since. There was not then, and there is not now, any real logic to my putting style. Frequently I will change my grip over two putts on the same green. Often I will take a practice swing with my hands in the normal grip and change them round when I stand over the ball. My own belief is that the secret of putting is to feel comfortable over the ball. Some days I look down at my hands and they do not feel right and so I change them round. It is all to do with feel. Within two years of my second putting breakdown I had resolved the problem to the extent that statistics suggested I was the best putter in Europe.

Yet the image remains, haunted by my early putting

problems. It is the Press - whether newspapers and magazines, radio or TV - who create the public image and they just will not let go. In the USA, for example, they constantly state that Raymond Floyd is a tremendous pressure player but he blows it as often as anyone else. With me it is that I am a bad putter. Almost every time I'm faced with a short putt some TV commentator will point out that this is my bad distance and millions of viewers will believe him.

I don't want to give the impression that I am anti Press. On the contrary I appreciate that they have a job to do and I also realize their importance. I like to think I am friends with some of the Press but as with any group of people there are some I prefer not to have anything to do with. I must confess that I am the sort of person who cannot easily forgive someone who criticizes unfairly.

Thus there is an editor of a British golf magazine who is not on my Christmas card list and there is a German journalist with whom I will not cooperate. The magazine editor criticized me unfairly some years ago when just one telephone call to check out his facts would have made him think again. Instead his words are read by many thousands of people and repeated in other publications until his 'facts' become the truth and my truth becomes a feeble excuse. The German reporter upset me when he wrote a terrible piece criticizing my behaviour after I had allowed him to caddy for me in one event. It was all nonsense but once again the damage was done once he went into print. At least, in this instance, I had the chance of a litle revenge when a few years ago *Playboy* requested an interview and I agreed until I learned this same reporter was to do the piece. I refused, cost him a fair amount of money and happily contemplated the fact that the wheel does turn full circle.

Mostly, though, I have been grateful for the press I

have received over the years. Golf writers seem less concerned than some sports reporters with the scandalous side of life. Most are genuine fans of golf and I intend to enjoy a healthy, working relationship with them all for many years to come.

6

A rival called Seve

Life since 1982 could not have been much better for Bernhard Langer. After finally sorting out his putting he has gone from strength to strength, from record payday to record payday. Even in his last great trial year of 1982 he finished the season sixth in Europe after winning £48,088. Just a few years later that amount of money seems like peanuts compared to what Langer can earn. The secret of success is timing and in Bernhard's case his timing could hardly have been keener. As his own talent grew, so did public interest in golf take off around the world. Increased leisure time, greater affiuence and the influence of television com-

bined to give the game a kick in the pants that was reflected in every player's wallet.

While these factors provide the platform for a sport to take off it takes more for a game to sustain its appeal. In short, it takes heroes. Sports fans do not want to watch someone doing something that they too could do if only they had taken the time to practise. No, what is required is someone who can do what the fan not only cannot do but what he or she could never even imagine attempting. Throughout its history golf has been fortunate in having a succession of great champions who have led by example.

By the time Langer rose to prominence himself, the latest in this glittering line was the Spaniard Severiano Ballesteros. The two men were born just four months apart in 1957 – Seve is the older – and since 1981 their careers have been linked; each judged by the other, each with his own legion of supporters. The contrast in their styles, with Langer studious and careful against Ballesteros's go-for-it philosophy, was as dramatically different as their physical appearance. While Ballesteros reacted to success or failure with widely different emotions etched on his face, the phlegmatic German always seemed in control. It was inevitable that a Press hungry for personal confrontation in golf should begin to set the two stars against each other. Even the most enthusiastic reporter could not have hoped for what happened in August of 1981 when Langer sat on a three-man panel to decide whether Seve should be selected for that year's Ryder Cup team. The decision made that day was not only to make headlines around the world, it was to affect for years the relationship between the two men.

The meeting that was to decide whether Seve was in the 1981 Ryder Cup team was held during the week of the Benson and Hedges International at Fulford Golf Club,

just outside York. The tournament is always staged in
August so usually good weather can be expected even in
an English summer. Yet as I made my way to the
meeting, with Ryder Cup captain John Jacobs and PGA
European Tour chairman Neil Coles, I felt even hotter
than everyone else around me. I was there as leader in
the Money List and for weeks players had been
discussing which way the vote should go.

Normally there would have been no problem. Seve
was without argument a great golfer, the star of the
European Tour and a man talented enough to walk into
any Ryder Cup team in history. And yet...

The problem was that he had been arguing with
officials all year. He had also taken part in a television
documentary which seemed to suggest at one point that
he owed golf nothing. Quite a few people felt he had
grown too big for his boots, that he needed to be taught a
lesson and that his inclusion would cause more upset to
other team members than it would do to weld the side
together. It was against this backdrop of gossip and
angry debate that the three of us met to decide Seve's
fate.

As everyone now knows we decided he should not be
selected. I am often asked which way I voted, what was
said and how the other two men felt about Seve. I have
always refused to talk about it and I am not about to do
anything different. As far as I am concerned that
meeting was a private affair. Of course, the outcome
was public but what actually happened behind closed
doors and between the three of us remains a secret. I
would be betraying something if I revealed what
happened. As it is no one knows for sure who voted for or
against Seve or indeed if *anyone* voted for him. All that
is known is that at least two people voted against him.

The decision, of course, made good copy for the
journalists and the Benson and Hedges event was

Top left: With my mother Wally at three months old

Top right: Anhausen's streets may not have been paved with gold, but in winter they did have snow. Here I am (*left*) sharpening my skiing technique

Above: They also serve who only pull the cart. Aged ten, I prepare for another day's work at Augsburg Country Club

The famous tree-iron shot that helped nudge my name all over the world. It was played by the 17th green during the 1981 Benson & Hedges International at Fulford, York

OPPOSITE

Top left: My first significant victory – the 1975 German Closed Championship – and a trophy big enough to impress anyone

Top right: A European Tour winner at last. A salver to savour – the 1980 Dunlop Masters at Chepstow

Bottom left: Happiness is holing a birdie putt in the 1979 Open Championship at Royal Lytham

Bottom right: Two's company. My long-time friend Manuel Pinero and I go to work on a putt during the 1981 Ryder Cup

Top: On my way to winning the 1981 Bob Hope Classic in England. Bob Hope, meanwhile, practises swimming without water

Above: The line-up for the 1982 US Masters International Players dinner at Augusta. Standing (*left to right*): Yutaka Hogawa, Philippe Ploujoux, Greg Norman, Peter Oosterhuis, Bernhard Langer, Dave Barr. (*Seated*): Isao Aoki, Gary Player, Hord Hardin (Masters chairman), Seve Ballesteros, David Graham

OPPOSITE

Top left: No matter what the game, the secret is to concentrate on the ball. Soccer is another of my passions

Top right: Who's the Boss? With business manager John Simpson of the International Management Group

Bottom: And then there were four. With my then fiancée Vikki, my mother Wally and father Erwin a few weeks before our wedding in 1984

Sometimes golf is not a funny game. With Ballesteros during our duel in the final of the 1984 World Matchplay Championship at Wentworth

OPPOSITE

Top left: Victory on the 18th green of the 1985 US Masters

Top right: This should fit you sir! Receiving the coveted Green Jacket from Ben Crenshaw at Augusta

Bottom: Making them laugh during my winner's speech at the 1985 US Masters

Top left: Disappointment as the pitch-shot that needed to go in to force a play-off in the 1985 Open just slips by the hole

Top right: Using technique and concentration to lead me to victory in the 1985 European Open at Sunningdale

Above: Who's looking after who? Wearing some novel headgear as I arrive on the 18th green on my way to winning the 1985 European Open

almost forgotten as the writers concentrated on our
Ryder Cup decision. Even though I was not very
experienced about the Press back then I was not stupid
and I knew that there would be a sensation. Even so, the
amount of space in the newspapers devoted to the
subject not just the next day but for weeks, months and,
I suppose, years came as a surprise.

Not that I was embarrassed by the decision. The fact
is that if Seve had played just one more tournament that
year he could have played himself into the side anyway.
It was his decision not to do that. You must also
remember that it was not just Severiano Ballesteros
who was on the agenda for discussion that day, but half
a dozen other hopefuls as well. Every player had been
trying very hard for several months to make the side
and each golfer had his own section of support. No
matter what we had decided we knew that someone
would be upset and that the critics would have a field
day. If we had selected Seve, for example, then I'm sure
some members of the media would have claimed that he
was king of the European Tour and that he could do
whatever he wanted and get away with it. For Neil
Coles, John Jacobs and myself it was a no-win
situation. The outcry was set up anyway.

Nowadays, Tony Jacklin has insisted that he alone
picks the last three players to make the side. This does
not make it a perfect system but at least it does mean
that a player is not put in the situation I found myself in
back in 1981 when I had to sit in judgement on a fellow
professional. Looking back now I feel the decision was
wrong. The argument that he was the single most
talented golfer available to the side is irrefutable.
Probably that consideration should have won the day
for him. But this is all hypothesis. All I know for certain
is that it seemed to affect our relationship.

I had known Seve since I first came on the tour in

1976. At that time I spoke no English but I did have a smattering of Spanish and the Spanish players were very kind to me. Men like Manuel Pinero, Antonio Garrido, Manuel Calero and Jose-Maria Canizares went out of their way to make me welcome and to invite me to dine with them in the long evenings that follow a day's play. By then Seve had been on the tour for a couple of years and he was already marked out as someone different. Even then he had a sort of star quality in everything he did that was impressive.

In some ways we were very similar, in others we were starkly different. As we are the same age it might seem logical that we would become friends immediately. We had both learned to play golf the hard way with a single club and, mostly, on our own. Seve, however, came from a family steeped in golf and its traditions whereas my own family knew little or nothing about the game and its possibilities. His brothers were all professional players and they and the other Spaniards on tour protected him like a rare bloom. They recognized his potential and so he was cocooned in this travelling family.

Success came for him almost immediately so that he was a big name, a star, almost before he was grown up. While I was still aiming to make a cut, he was going for victory. By the time his career had taken off and was climbing steadily towards rarified heights, my own game was lucky to be still in existence. Yet I have never seen him as a rival because in golf I do not believe that anyone can stop me winning except myself. Apart from matchplay, it is me against the course.

Instead I have always admired him and always been happy to watch him play the game. I can understand the media and the public making us rivals because it is always more exciting when two men are fighting for the top spot consistently, like Nicklaus and Palmer did for so many years. But the truth is different.

As far as I am concerned Seve is a truly great golfer. He is one of the best in the world and certainly the most natural golfer I have ever seen. At times in his career he has played the game on a different level to anyone else. When he won the Open at Royal Lytham in 1979, for example, he was simply brilliant. Some Americans labelled him 'lucky' after that victory because of one shot out of a car park, but that is nonsense. One shot does not win an Open, only a succession of brilliant ones can do that and Seve in 1979 was breathtaking in his play.

Even now Seve is one of the very few players I will stop to watch on the practice ground. Many players I refuse to watch because their action can give me bad mental pictures to take out on the course but that is never so with Ballesteros. He has a great rhythm, he is very fluent and his swing is not a series of compensations for one mistake after another. There is a fluidity about him that is fantastic. He simply seems to flow into a shot. Contrast him and Greg Norman, for example, and you will see that whereas Greg appears to be giving everything 100 per cent, Seve plays with much less effort and looks much smoother. Yet he hits the ball almost as far.

Apart from his natural talent, I am convinced this sweet rhythm and sound technique come from years of playing in Spain. Whereas I could play only seven months a year before winter set in, Seve could practise and play for 12 months *and* on a better course. On the debit side I suppose that meant he lost more of his childhood than I did but then everything in life has a price. I often think about the fact that Seve, Nick Faldo, Sandy Lyle and myself are all the same age and I like to imagine these four little boys practising golf in different parts of Europe and then coming together to contest the world's great titles through the eighties.

Despite my instinctive and abiding admiration for Seve, we have never become close friends. Even as young men we rarely had dinner together or went out for an evening. There was no animosity, just a gap. Maybe that is just the way fate decided we must be.

Although I was happy to accept this as a fact of life, I was very unhappy with what happened after he had been left out of the 1981 Ryder Cup side. Now in place of the gap between us there was a discernible coldness. Suddenly Seve became remote when I was around and the chill that hung in the air was upsetting. I suppose it was a situation that could not go on forever without something happening. This 'something' came during the 1984 World Matchplay Championships at Wentworth.

Both of us love Wentworth. The course seems to suit our games because we have both played some outstanding golf on the West Course. In 1984 we were both in excellent form and, against a breathtaking backdrop of English autumnal colours, we made our way through to the final itself. It was a match that caught the imagination of the public and the reporters who had gathered at Wentworth. After making certain of my final place on the Saturday afternoon I went to the usual Press conference, an event that was more concerned about my date with Seve the next day than about the golf I had just played to get there.

It was during the course of this interview that I said I did not much like playing with Seve because he intimidated his fellow goifers on the course. I did not mean to infer that he was deliberately intimidating anyone but that is how most of the reporters interpreted my remark and it made banner headlines in every Sunday newspaper. Before arriving at Wentworth that morning I read the stories myself and realized that Seve would almost certainly see them for himself. When he arrived he was even cooler than usual. He carried out the required niceties but only just and I realized that this was going to be a very difficult day. In the end it was not only difficult but disappointing as I lost 2 and 1.

While I was still digesting my defeat and analyzing where I had gone wrong I was asked to attend the Press conference. Normally the new champion talks to reporters first at Wentworth and then exits while his defeated opponent comes in for a much shorter interview. This time Seve stayed in the Press Tent and as I walked towards the front of the interview area I could feel the atmosphere closing in around me. Without even waiting for me to sit down, Seve stood and asked me what I meant by saying he tried to intimidate other players. He had been geed up by the reporters, of course, and he looked not so much furious as shocked. I recall saying quietly that I had not meant to say this, that I did not believe it and that there was no need for an argument. A potentially explosive situation was defused and the cameramen who had focused on us in case there was a violent row, retreated disappointed. Even so it was not a pleasant moment and I realized we could not go on like this.

Ever since 1981 I had suspected that Seve had held the Ryder Cup decision against me in a curiously personal way. If so, I could understand his hurt and his resentment and now, after this latest and public incident at Wentworth, I knew the time was right to have it out with him. My comment to the reporters about his intimidation on the course had been meant to describe his attitude. Part of Seve's success can be explained by his ability to cocoon himself in steely concentration so that he appears sometimes not to notice with whom he is playing. He rarely comments on a rival's good shot, seldom does anything that might

possibly boost a playing partner's confidence. Perhaps
he sees this as a sign of weakness on his behalf but
whatever the reason it meant that playing with him
was, for me, sometimes difficult.

So I chose my moment when only the two of us were
around to ask if he felt there really was a problem
between us because of the Ryder Cup or because of
something else I had said or done. To my delight he
seemed genuinely surprised and insisted that he was
not harbouring any grudge and that he really did not
feel he treated me any differently from most other
players. In the end we had a good chat and I explained
to him that other players sometimes felt intimidated by
his mere presence, by the force of his personality. I
appreciated that this was not his fault but he should be
aware that it was not so much what he did, or did not do,
at times but simply because he *was* Seve that other
lesser mortals could feel pressure in his presence in the
heat of battle. The talk was extremely worthwhile. We
learned something about each other in the course of this
private conversation and suddenly the air was cleared
between us.

I told him that though we were two completely
different guys that there was, nonetheless, no reason
why there should be anything other than good
vibrations between us. The conversation worked, the
distance between us receded significantly and since
that day in 1984 our relationship has been much better.
Nowadays we play the occasional practice round
together, chat happily on the putting green and though
neither of us goes out of his way to seek the other's
company there is no significance in this. And, of course,
I still admire his golf and his talent.

I can understand why thousands of people go to
watch him play the game. Indeed I still enjoy doing the
same myself when the opportunity presents itself. It is

just that he is what he is and I am what I am. Maybe in the future we can become genuinely close friends. I hope so. Until then, however, fate has chosen to make us rivals. It is not necessarily a bad thing either for I believe this not only adds to the game of golf as a whole but it gives each of us a little extra edge whenever we get into contention at the same tournament.

Meanwhile, we are all growing older and, hopefully, a little wiser. Certainly Seve has mellowed with age. We should all become nicer, more understanding people as we mature and I have detected this change in Seve as I have - I hope - in myself too. Severiano Ballesteros is at heart a nice guy and I wish him only good luck for the future.

7

The Ryder what?

Growing up in Anhausen must have been a pleasant experience for Bernhard Langer. His home in this typically clean and tidy village, tucked in foothills several miles outside Munich, provided an ideal base for a young boy. It was safe to walk the streets. It still is. If he wanted to stroll in open country with the wind blowing in his face he only had to step outside his parents' home, leap over the brook that burbles through their back garden and head off into those hills. In many ways Anhausen was isolated from outside influences and this explains why Langer is so consumed with the idea of family life. It also explains why he knew so little of golf's history, its legends and heroes until he was almost ready himself to step into the game's fabric. By the turn of this century golf seems certain to be one of Germany's major sports but when Langer was a lad it was considered an almost eccentric pastime.

Certainly the Ryder Cup meant little if anything to either Bernhard Langer or anyone else in Anhausen. The situation would almost certainly have remained the same today were it not for the fact that as America's team yawned their way to yet another Ryder Cup success in the mid-seventies Jack Nicklaus got up off his hind legs and suggested it might be more serious fun if the side was selected not just from the best that Great Britain and Ireland could provide but from the Continental stars as well. Traditionalists bridled at the Nicklaus thought but the times were changing and when Seve Ballesteros emerged the scene was set for a change in the rules that turned Great Britain and Ireland into Europe. The first European team did little to alter the status quo, however, when they competed at The Greenbrier in West Virginia in 1979. Once again the Americans triumphed easily. Nor was there much difference two years later at Walton Heath when a supremely gifted American side easily defeated Europe. Slowly, however, the tide was turning towards Europe and in Langer's second Ryder Cup appearance in 1983 the belief began to dawn that America's supremacy was no longer to be regarded as one of life's harsher facts...

Before I joined the tour in 1976 I knew little if anything about the Ryder Cup. Golf in general was hardly a hot newspaper item in Germany at that time and the Ryder Cup itself was simply something that did not concern us. It did not take long, however, for me to realize the emotion and the concern this private competition between the British and the Irish and the Americans aroused every two years. I could hardly believe the tension and the effort experienced by good players in 1977 when they were trying to play their way into the team. At the time I recall wishing I could be a part of it all but as I was German that seemed as likely as captaining England at cricket.

Then the rules were changed to allow Continental players into the side and although I could not hope to make the first European side in 1979, I was determined to make it next time round in 1981. When I did just that I was thrilled. It was tremendously exciting to feel myself one of the best 24 players in the world that weekend at Walton Heath. Yet although I was delighted to be there I knew in my heart that we had practically no chance of beating the Americans that year.

If that comes across as defeatist then I apologize but before you criticize me too much allow me to recite the team they had assembled for the occasion. It reads: Lee Trevino, Tom Kite, Bill Rogers, Larry Nelson, Ben Crenshaw, Bruce Lietzke, Jerry Pate, Hale Irwin, Johnny Miller, Tom Watson, Raymond Floyd and Jack Nicklaus. That was the order in which they played the last day singles and these last three are no 'tail-end Charlies', believe me. Between them the Americans had more 'majors' than some armies can boast and it was little wonder that we wandered away slightly dazed after losing 18½-9½.

Two years later it was different. In the intervening months Sandy Lyle, Nick Faldo, and Ken Brown had matured and improved almost beyond belief. Suddenly there was a nucleus of gifted golfers in the European side. Suddenly we had a spine around which the new skipper Tony Jacklin could mount a creditable challenge. The Cup was contested at the PGA National in Florida and what a week it turned out to be. Most of us had played some US Tour events by then and we knew we could beat them if we played our best.

As I had never really been an amateur, I had had little experience of matchplay. After turning pro I was picked for a couple of Hennessey Cup sides but that was really the sum total of my knowledge of this form of golf. The 1981 Ryder Cup had showed me what a thrill it was to be part of a team and to play matchplay in front of big crowds. I loved it even though as a professional trying to earn a living from the game I would not want to play this style each week. Insanity, if not penury, lies at the end of that road.

But as our plane dipped into southern Florida I felt a growing sense of eager anticipation at what lay before me and my team-mates. If I had enjoyed losing in 1981, how would I feel if we could actually manage to beat the Americans in their own backyard? It was a delightful thought and the fact that the great Jack Nicklaus was now the American skipper only added to the sense of excitement.

Our own captain, Jacklin, was as yet untested in this great contest but the early signs were good. I had enjoyed playing under John Jacobs two years earlier. John is extremely knowledgeable about the game and the players and is a nice man. He is a good motivator as well but I knew Tony much better because he was still either playing tournament golf or around the golf scene at that time. It was easier for me to relate to him. Tony also has a terrific personality. Looked at from any angle he is an impressive man and the fact that he had won the Open Championships of both Britain and America meant he had been there himself before us.

In 1979 the Ryder Cup side had travelled to America in the economy section of a British Airways flight. Jacklin, however, insisted that we not only fly first class but that we fly Concorde. In the last three Ryder Cups his captaincy has been marked by an insistence that the

players came first and last in every consideration.
Nothing was too good for us but it took someone of
Jacko's forceful personality to get the point across.
Psychologically it was first-rate thinking on his part.
From the moment we gathered together as a team he
worked on increasing our self-esteem... and he suc-
ceeded brilliantly.

I have played for Tony in three Ryder Cup sides now
and I can honestly say I have never heard him utter a
negative word. He discusses everything with us,
encourages us to have our say and insists that we meet
at least once every day as a team. All he asks is that we
do our best out on the course. And it is our pleasure to do
just that.

Even Tony, however, cannot do anything about the
weather, and in 1983 in Florida it was foul. Soaring
temperatures and searing humidity combined to make
it an effort just to walk the course, never mind play golf
and concentrate hard at the same time. By the time I'd
walked from the locker room to the practice tee I was
already dripping with sweat, my shirt hanging limply
from my shoulders.

Despite the weather, despite the fact that the PGA
National is about as classically American a course as
you can get, we very nearly overcame all the odds that
week. As we went into the last day's singles the two
teams were locked together at eight points each and it
looked as though a shock to equal the earlier capture of
the America's Cup by Australia in 1983 was on the
cards. America's sporting inheritance was on the line
and both they and ourselves knew it.

In the end we just lost out. They took 6½ points from
the 12 available on the last day and won 14½-13½. Tom
Watson won the last match against Bernard Gallacher
with a bogey at the 17th. It was desperately disappointing and yet at the same time uplifting, a curious mixture

of emotions. We left Florida feeling that we should have won but *knowing* for the first time that we could have won. The Americans had been shown that we were no longer pushovers and the scene was set for one of the greatest weeks of my life in 1985.

For months before the contest at The Belfry, near Birmingham in England, the Press had been building up this Ryder Cup as the one we would win. The hype was fantastic and no one, least of all the players, was immune from it. Like some contagious disease the thought that we could win turned into a belief that we would triumph for the first time since 1957.

Yet when at last the actual week came and we all moved into the team HQ at The Belfry Hotel, the pressure came tumbling down on our shoulders, like rain out of a clear, blue sky. I had always experienced more pressure in the Ryder Cup than in any other tournament. At least if I blew a Masters or an Open because I missed a few short putts the only person I was really letting down was myself. But in a Ryder Cup you feel desperately that you don't want to disappoint teammates. Everyone says to each other that it doesn't matter but we all feel the same. When you triumph, then this feeling adds measurably to the feeling of elation – but when you lose it makes everything so much harder to bear.

Suddenly at The Belfry as we practised and discussed various partnerships I realized that this time we had the added burden of an expectant public on our shoulders as well. For the first time I appreciated the mixture of anticipation and dread that must accompany a soccer team as they prepare to leave the dressing room to play in a big match.

Once again, however, Jacklin was terrific. He was everywhere that week, like some turbo-charged mother hen, looking after us, cocooning us from as much hassle as possible and all the time quietly stressing that we had the ability to beat the American side. Lee Trevino was the opposition captain and, though he arrived with his usual jester's smile firmly in place, it was noticeable that as the first day edged nearer, laughing Lee began to look more and more serious.

Lee was smiling after the opening foursome matches at The Belfry, however, for the Americans won three points to our one. I partnered Nick Faldo and we lost 3 and 2 against Calvin Peete and Tom Kite. Only Seve Ballesteros and Manuel Pinero won. It was not the start we had been looking for and back in the Press tent reporters glanced back over their stories in that morning's papers when they predicted a great home victory and began to construct plausible excuses. They also, quite probably, cursed us for fooling them.

Yet as was to happen two years later, we came back in the afternoon fourball matches, winning 2½ to 1½. This time I partnered Jose-Maria Canizares – Faldo had told Jacklin he was not really playing well enough to carry on – and we got a half against Craig Stadler and Hal Sutton. So we finished the day behind by one point, 3½ to 4½. The next morning's fourball matches were to prove crucial.

Once again I had a different partner, this time Sandy Lyle, and we played Craig Stadler and Curtis Strange in the last of the morning pairings. Players sometimes ask for a specific partner or suggest to the captain that they would prefer not to play with so and so but it was purely coincidental that I had changed partners for every dance. By the time our match reached the 18th green Europe had won two of the earlier matches and lost one so the overall match was all square.

Sandy and I, however, were one hole down as we played that 18th and when Stadler was left standing over a two and a half foot putt which he only needed to hole for a half at the last hole, our fate seemed to be sealed. Instead Stadler missed this short putt, we halved our match and the delight ran through the entire team. It was a turning point. The Americans seemed under pressure for the first time and their reputation as a team of supermen who could do no wrong on the greens was shredded.

Some people have expressed surprise that Sandy and I asked Stadler to knock in such a short putt. It was at least two and a half feet and it was left to right. Under the circumstances it was no 'gimme'. In fact, neither Sandy nor I even looked at each other to confirm that Stadler should have to hole it. If I had been in the American's position then I would have expected to have to putt out. Even so I expected him to make it and for us to lose by one hole. It was a pleasant surprise when he missed even though we both felt sorry for him, knowing what he felt as he slumped over his club on that green. I'm only glad that he has recovered from that moment and remains a power in golf because, believe me, one incident like that, under that sort of intense public scrutiny, can easily fracture a personality.

So instead of losing a whole point, we had gained a half for our team and the difference, not only in the score, but in our confidence as a team was deeply significant. That afternoon I changed partners once again, this time joining Ken Brown, and we beat Ray Floyd and Lanny Wadkins - the Americans' anchor-team - 3 and 2. It meant that Europe took a two-point lead into the final day's singles and it was the signal for the most emotional day I've ever spent on a golf course.

Right from the start there was an air of expectancy hanging over The Belfry. It was like being at the very centre of a huge party as the TV cameras started zooming in on the action and the spectators filled the course so that the only easy place to walk was on the fairways themselves. The Americans never really stood a chance as fans and players combined to form one huge team. Individual ambitions had been tossed away in favour of a collective will to succeed.

No one captured the spirit of that day better than my Spanish friend Manuel Pinero who was chosen to play in the first and most crucial match. Trevino had selected Wadkins for this opening battle in the belief that Lanny was the most formidable matchplayer in the American game. If anyone could shift the balance of power Uncle Sam's way then it would be Lanny.

Manuel, however, was inspired that day. When Jacklin announced the pairings the evening before Pinero had let out a whoop of delight that he had drawn Wadkins and then announced very seriously to Tony that he would beat his opponent. When news of his 3 and 1 victory swept back through the field on the final afternoon, it was received by each of us as a symbol of our ultimate destiny.

There were scoreboards all over the place and it was relatively easy to keep track of events even though over the last few hours of a Ryder Cup things can change swifter than an English summer's day. Even without these scoreboards it was no problem to feel which side was winning. The cheers that went up as the European team secured another hole or another actual win, erupted constantly like so many small, joyful explosions all over the course. It was like being on a giant roller-coaster ride... slightly scary but very exciting.

My own match went well and I managed to beat Hal Sutton 5 and 4. That meant I'd finished my day's work early enough to hurtle around the last few holes encouraging team-mates and witnessing the action. By the time Sam Torrance came to the 18th green and holed a wonderful birdie putt to beat Andy North I was in the crowd of players and officials watching this historic moment as the Ryder Cup was won.

Sam - a nice man, a quiet man and a man whose reputation suggests he is a tough man as well - had tears in his eyes even before his putt went into the hole. So did I. So did we all. The crowd went wild and we were carried away on a storm of emotion and happiness. I recall Concorde twice doing a victory fly-past over the hotel and the course, making the ground tremble and everyone's heart swell with pride.

The crowd refused to disperse for what seemed like hours afterwards. They gathered outside the hotel and chanted for Jacklin, for Seve, for Sam and for each one of us until we appeared on the roof of the pro's shop where we sprayed champagne over each other and anyone unwise enough to get within drenching distance. It was all good-natured stuff and it continued into the dinner and the impromptu party later that night. A wonderful, wonderful day.

Yet there had been some less than wonderful things about that day as well. Before the American side flew back home, my singles opponent Hal Sutton had criticized the crowd's behaviour, claiming that they were unsporting in their behaviour and that he had been shocked and upset at the way in which poor, or unlucky, American shots had been jeered or cheered.

Hal's was the only criticism quoted in the papers the following day but I know that most of the Americans felt the same and I must say I have some sympathy for them. Some of them appreciated the occasion better than others and realized just how much this win meant to the British crowd that day but they were still upset about it. The Brits have always been known for their sportsmanship and the fact that they are knowledge-able enough about golf to applaud a really good shot and to keep their mouths shut when someone mistimes a stroke or makes a hash of a difficult shot.

This was not the case at The Belfry and there were times when I felt embarrassed about what was going on out there. I didn't feel great to see and to hear some sections of the crowd behave the way they did that day. But the support they gave *us* was fantastic. I think some people just got a bit carried away by it all. The herd instinct took over. Many of them had been waiting for 28 years to witness a Ryder Cup victory and now on this fabulous day in Sutton Coldfield, all that pent-up emotion came tumbling out. Still, it seems a pity that some people have labelled Hal a bad loser just because he had the courage to mention it.

After the victory comes the let-down. This feeling of emptiness was more acute than ever after the Ryder Cup. It was for me the first time I'd taken part in a victorious team event and the euphoria that comes with an experience that is shared had been delightful. Now, like the others, I felt low. It is the same feeling that encourages mountaineers to climb again. The joy, you see, is in getting there, of making the climb. Once you have stood on the peak there is nowhere to go but down – until you graft your way towards the next peak, of course.

As far as the Ryder Cup was concerned I had to wait, like everyone else, for another two years before that particular peak rose before me. In 1987 we played at Muirfield Village in Ohio, the home state of Jack Nicklaus. Jack was also appointed skipper of the U S A, a sure sign that they were determined to rub our noses in the dirt this time, and it was not made any easier by choosing Jack's own course, the memorial he has built to himself and his golfing ideals, as the battleground.

Once again we flew in by Concorde and once again the British Press began banging the drum on our behalf long before the first ball was struck at Muirfield Village. The pressure, if anything, was even greater than it had been at The Belfry. Under Nicklaus's shrewd leadership the American golfing public was made more aware than ever before that a Ryder Cup was taking place. For the first time there was prime-time TV coverage and all the major papers and magazines arrived to report over the three days.

According to the European reporters we arrived feeling confident that we would successfully defend the trophy. That was the impression we wanted to convey obviously but the truth was somewhat different. We knew only too well that we had never won over there and we realized just how hard the Americans would be trying to defeat us. Their pride was at stake and the Americans have a lot of pride.

If we were not as confident as we pretended then I must say the Americans were over-confident. They really thought it was going to be no big deal to give us a hiding on a course they knew so well, a track that had been set up by Jack to meet their every requirement. There was just one exception to this general rule; the fairways were a little wider than is usual in the States and this little bit of width suited us perhaps more than our opponents.

Even so, the Americans' confidence did not appear misplaced after a couple of hours' play on the first morning. After nine holes' play in each of the four matches we were three down in the top match, three down in the second, four down in the third and two down in the fourth. It could have been worse – but not much worse. Disaster beckoned. All the big words before this Ryder Cup had begun now began to gather round our necks like so many millstones.

I was playing poorly. My partner, Ken Brown, was not playing well either. It was a struggle. Ahead of us we could see that Sam Torrance and Howard Clark were not doing much better. Behind us Nick Faldo and Ian

Woosnam looked down .if not yet out. It required something special for us to get out of this mess. Suddenly Woosnam and Faldo found their game, while Seve and Jose-Maria Olazabal in the last match began to pick up good vibrations from what was happening in front of them. Instead of losing all four morning foursomes, we won two of them. Once again, as with Stadler's missed putt two years previously, the Americans were stunned at their own inability to turn the screw.

From then on the whole thing sped past like a wonderful dream. We won all four points in the afternoon fourballs and by the time the second day's play came to an end we were ahead by five points. Surely nothing could stop us now. Jack Nicklaus looked drained as he watched his men fall over one after another and the American TV commentators struggled to describe what was happening to the cream of their nation's golfers in their own backyard. And out on the course itself the atmosphere had changed dramatically.

On the first day the American crowd had been impeccably behaved. Largely unused to watching matchplay anyway they had been polite and appreciative of good shots from either side. Overnight their mood changed. In place of genteel applause we were suddenly offered naked patriotism. I recall on the second morning being amazed as I walked to the first tee to see and hear a gang of women chanting each American player's name like some overgrown group of high school cheerleaders. The Stars and Stripes were everywhere. It was like being surrounded by the enemy. If we'd had wagons we would have pulled them into a circle immediately.

The 'cheerleaders' kept their singing up all day like a nagging headache that wouldn't go away. They were quite good at it actually, but terribly noisy and I was

shocked to hear them act like that on a golf course. It
just wasn't in keeping with the occasion. When I made
that first tee I said to an American official standing
there: 'They'll do anything to get on television, won't
they?' He turned away in embarrassment and disbelief.
It was only later that I discovered that one of the main
'cheerleaders' was his wife.

By now, however, the Americans were on a loser and I
even managed to shut up those chanting women with
what turned out to be the last shot of the day. It came as
shadows fell over the course and my partner Sandy Lyle
and I battled to protect the one-hole lead we carried on to
the 18th tee against Wadkins and Larry Nelson. We all
hit good tee shots but mine was the longest. Larry hit
first and made the green. Then Sandy knocked his ball
in and got a terrific cheer so we knew his ball was
reasonably close. We couldn't see how close, however,
because the green is tiered and we were beneath the flag.

Then Wadkins, the old gunslinger, blurred into
action. He had just birdied the previous two holes and at
first I thought he was going to eagle this one as his ball
flew straight at the flag. As it hit the green – out of sight
to us – there was an even bigger response than Sandy's
ball had received and I thought he must be closer, much
closer. I just remember thinking that one of us was
going to have to make a birdie to hold on to our lead.

I had about 150 yards left to the green and for me that
means an eight iron. It had been a long and a hard day
but my concentration was still good. I'd enjoyed the
morning foursomes when Sandy and I had beaten
Wadkins and Nelson and I didn't want to let anything
slip away now. We had been a good team together,
Sandy and I, for when I made a bit of a mess of a hole he
would step in to tidy up and I had managed to do the
same for him.

I knew I'd made good contact with the ball and I could

see that it was heading for the flag, like Wadkins' ball
had done a minute previously. What I didn't know was
that my ball struck the green and stopped quickly,
inches from the hole, whereas Lanny's had run on. Once
again a great cheer split the evening stillness. Out of my
sight behind the green, Jacko and Seve and Angel
Gallardo - an outstanding Spanish golfer of the pre-
Ballesteros era - were publicly going quite daft.
Meanwhile, back on the fairway I was trying to keep
calm, to hold my concentration for the birdie attempt I
felt sure I would still have to make. When Larry and
Lanny saw how close I was, however, they conceded the
putt. I was delighted. Without doubt - given the
circumstances - I had just struck the best shot of my life.
No matter what happens in the future I will never be
more content with a shot than I was with that one.

Nicklaus, typically, refused to contemplate defeat
even at this stage. Despite our five-point advantage, he
cajoled and coerced his players into giving one last
great effort in the final day's singles. And it nearly
worked. Until Eamon Darcy beat Ben Crenshaw by
holing a real 'knee-trembler' of a putt on the 18th green,
the Americans were moving within touching distance
of a remarkable sporting comeback. Eamon simply
stemmed the flow of European blood with that single
putt. The next match on to the 18th was my own against
Larry Nelson. We had been drawn together for the third
match in a row and we had enjoyed a fabulous match so
that we were all-square playing up the last.

After three more shots Larry was about two feet from
the hole and I was a couple of inches closer. Nothing
was certain on the super-fast greens that Nicklaus had
prepared at Muirfield that week, but as I walked
towards the balls I was reminded of something Jack
himself had done years previously. That was in the 1969
Ryder Cup at Royal Birkdale and in the last single
match Jack had conceded a missable putt to Tony

Jacklin so that the two sides finished with 16 points each. This happened before I had even heard of the Ryder Cup but it was a story built into the folklore of the game and, though I understand some of Jack's team-mates were not too happy with his decision, many hundreds of thousands of golf fans applauded his sportsmanship that afternoon.

Now as I walked towards Larry I felt that it would be a shame if either of us lost our match because of one silly, missed putt. I believed that it was entirely within the spirit of the match to offer a half. I also knew that this half point would guarantee we retained the trophy because it meant that the Americans could not actually defeat us. At best they could only halve the match. I don't think Larry realized this but this was not why I did it. It was, instead, just a gesture of friendship towards a very good friend and he agreed without question.

A few minutes later Seve Ballesteros beat Curtis Strange 2 and 1. We had done it. Against all the odds we had beaten America in America. Once again I enjoyed the unique feeling of achievement and joy that I had first experienced two years earlier at The Belfry. We sang, we danced, we cried. And the 3000 fans who had come from Europe to cheer us on did the same. While Olazabal danced a paso doble on the 18th green, I grinned a few feet away and waved a tiny German flag.

Twenty-four hours later when the team and officials arrived at London's Heathrow Airport the reception was fantastic. I have never known anything like it. It was as though The Beatles had come back to town. Just fantastic. In fact, it was almost frightening how many people were waiting to greet us and to cheer the golden chalice we had defended successfully in America. Sheer, blissful pandemonium reigned and once again I found a supreme high.

As I think again about these events, just a few months

later the euphoria is still high. Soon after our victory Jacklin spoke about what it would mean to the European Tour, how money would pour in, interest continue to escalate. And he was right. Throughout the eighties European golf has grown in strength, in talent, in money and in prestige so that the graph of success is almost vertical. Now we must battle harder than ever before to maintain growth. Perhaps it is unrealistic to expect such dramatic improvement to continue at this rate but it is essential that, as a Tour, we must not lose ground.

We went to the States determined, win or lose, to prove that 1985 was not a fluke, that the balance of power had tilted in our favour and that no matter what happens in the future the Ryder Cup will always be a close-fought affair. And a friendly and enjoyable one, too. We must, however, keep our feet firmly on the ground no matter how many stars we have in our eyes.

European golf is not as strong as the American Tour. Perhaps it never will be because their tour is longer, their conditions better, their supply of top-class players apparently inexhaustible. The fact is that if our top 50 players took on their top 50 then we would not stand a chance. They could throw out their top 10 golfers and bring in the next 10 and there would not be a world of difference. The same is not true of us and only a fanatic would think otherwise. This is not meant to be carping because I am very proud of our achievements but we must be realistic. I am very proud of our advancement in the world of golf. I am also sure that winning the Ryder Cup twice in a row has helped to make all this possible.

Unfortunately the actual arrangements for the Ryder Cup are not always as perfect as the event itself. For example, some people make a big deal out of the clothes and equipment we are offered for the Ryder Cup but this means little or nothing to me and it is the same for the majority of the players. I have my own clothing contract with Boss and I will never wear any of the sweaters, trousers or shirts again. For the Ryder Cup in America I blacked out the manufacturer's name and I wore my own shoes and gloves.

This was seen in some quarters as an act of petulance. It was not. It was self-protection. In 1985 several players lost lucrative contracts because they were pictured in advertisements promoting a Ryder Cup supplier. Now playing for the honour is one thing – since 1981 the players have been paid nothing – but when it actually starts to cost players hard-earned contracts then surely there is something wrong.

So I found it annoying when, on the day I arrived back in Germany from the 1987 Ryder Cup, I picked up a newspaper and there was a full page advert, a large picture of me and the name of the whisky company who were the main sponsors of the competition. I was aghast. Apart from anything else I have no wish to promote an alcoholic product.

I was not the only one upset. Three of my main sponsors – and I am referring to long-term contracts of up to 10 years – contacted me to say they were not pleased at this association. I could only apologize and point out that I knew nothing about it either. When I complained, I was told that the whisky people had a contract whereby they could use a team picture along with their brand name. They were not supposed to use a picture of an individual player. It was wrong but it was a *fait accompli*. The damage was done.

The fact is that I cannot make a living out of the Ryder Cup. Some believe that a player's contracts are improved automatically by Ryder selection but this is not so in my case. The Ryder Cup is now not worth 10 pennies to me one way or the other and I will not have it threaten my long-term security. Hopefully, things will be handled differently in 1989.

However, I do not wish to finish this personal odyssey through the Ryder Cup on a sour note. The fact is that the last two meetings with the U S A rank alongside my first Tour win and victory in the U S Masters in terms of sheer enjoyment. There are some wonderful memories to carry with me through the rest of my life.

A journalist - not a million miles removed from the one who has assisted me with this book - once asked Tony Jacklin if victory in the Ryder Cup would mean more to him than anything else he had done. This was in 1984 and Jacko's reply was: 'Don't be daft. I've won a British and a U S Open title.' Minutes after the winning putt dropped at Muirfield in 1987 Tony was asked for his reaction by a TV commentator. He started to speak, broke up and then stepped back from the microphone, muttering: 'I'm sorry, this has been the greatest day of my life.' Daft, eh? I know precisely what he means and one day I hope to be a Ryder Cup captain myself and to experience what Tony has enjoyed as our skipper over the last couple of years.

8

The money game

As Langer climbed towards the more rarified heights of golf through the eighties, so his earning capacity increased. The speed at which money was hurled at him is a tribute not only to an astute management but to the golfing boom in Europe. Cash, ready cash, has always been available to golf's stars but in recent years the endorsements have moved outside the obvious ones of clubs and golf clothing and into a commercial world eager to attach their product's name to the right sporting star. As ever in this hard-headed world, image has been vital. It is necessary to be a winner, of course, but it is even more important to be seen as the right sort

of winner. Langer is now, and always has been, aware
of his image. He guards this personal picture carefully.
As a person he is dependable, he is modest and he is
forthright. In public he is the same. The Langer you
might meet on a plane is the same guy as the star who
strides the world's fairways. In this case, at least, what
you see is what you get.

   Since 1978 he has been handled by the International
Management Group - the Mark McCormack sports
agency which controls the financial destiny of many of
the world's top sportsmen and women and which also is
an important, powerful factor in the PGA European
Tour. More than one European event is the brainchild of
IMG and the group's influence extends far beyond
merely lining up contracts for famous clients. The IMG
European golf division is headed in London by John
Simpson. Simpson believes in a close relationship with
his golfers.

   It is Simpson's job to take a client like Langer and to
make an appropriate commercial connection. He
stresses that they never look for a 'quick' buck but that
instead they are concerned with a long-term attach-
ment. 'It means looking for what I like to call "blue-
chip" companies,' explains Simpson. 'A guy like
Bernhard is going to be around for a very long time so
there is no point getting involved with companies who
might not even be trading in a few years. The
interesting thing about Bernhard is that he takes an
active interest in everything we do. Some players
couldn't care less and leave it all to us. But not Bernhard
– he wants to know everything. And he wants to know it
all the time.' It is an attitude that has made Langer one
of the richest sportsmen in the world.

I have a rough idea of how much money I have but I
have a precise idea of what I'm worth commercially. It

is important to draw the distinction. At first, like anyone else, I merely wanted to play golf for a living. Now I find that several people's livelihood depends upon how I play golf. The pressure to play well has always been there but now it comes from a different direction.

Ever since 1978 I have been with I M G and I have never regretted the association. I'll never know if I could have made more money by promoting myself but I doubt it. Like any other successful organization I M G have their critics. Some people claim their influence is too big, that they can squeeze certain parts of the golf world until they get what they want. Personally I cannot agree with this. As far as I can see, I M G have been innovative and created much that has been not only of benefit to themselves but to others as well. Certainly they have made mistakes along the way but then that is true of everyone. To be human is to err occasionally.

My own earnings have leapfrogged throughout the eighties. First I had to become a winner. Then, having overcome that obstacle, I became number one in Europe. And then there was the U S Masters title. At each of these three points my fame spread a little further and, as my consistency improved, so companies were able to look on me as a long-term investment. It means that today I have several major contracts with world-famous companies. These are: a contract with Wilson golf clubs, with American Express, with Mercedes cars and with Boss, the German clothing company.

In each case I have got involved not only because the contract was right but because I can honestly recommend the product. Wilson make super clubs and I have even designed my own range – the Bernhard Langer Autograph Club – that was launched at the beginning of 1987. Neither American Express nor Mercedes need any explanation as to their excellence while the Boss clothes I wear both on and off the golf course are the sort of clothes I would buy for myself. The strand connecting these four companies is, I suppose, the pursuit of excellence. As ever, it does not come cheap.

Apart from these major contracts, which range from two to five years, I have contracts with Adidas (golf shoes), Ebel watches, Lufthansa and a Japanese clothing range called 'The Masters' but which I only wear when I am competing in Japan. Usually the agreement means I am required to do a certain amount of company days. This means the company involved arranges for their more important customers to come to a golf course where they are entertained both on and off the course. My job is to mingle, to give a clinic and, sometimes, to play.

I try to give good value in each case. I think I have the right image and I try hard to come over pretty good to people, to make contact with them. Whether it is at a company day or during a tournament I try to be the same. I believe in politeness, in honesty and in sincerity. If someone wants an autograph then I try to oblige. You see, I don't like arrogant or rude people myself. It costs nothing to be pleasant.

Yes, I'm proud of my image. It has taken a long time for this image to be created. By that I don't mean it is artificial, just that it takes people a long time to feel they know you. Lots of things combine to create this image. The Press, television, radio and, of course, word of mouth. In my own case, there was the time I climbed a tree to play a shot in the Benson and Hedges tournament at Fulford in England. At the time it seemed the only sensible thing to do but it also made marvellous television and photographs of the incident appeared all over the world. Now I cannot claim to have deliberately hit my ball up the tree - would that I had that much talent! - but my response to it helped turn me from just another golfer into something of a personality.

It has been the same with clothing. I like bright colours and modern styles and Boss have created a range that not only looks and feels good but which makes me stand out from the crowd. At the same time I have tried not to offend anyone and to do the right thing. I try to be punctual, to do my job and to be polite. I hope others do the same.

Money has never been the real motivation for me. I realize this always sounds corny when someone relatively rich says it but it is the truth. The fact is that if I get my golf right and conduct my life properly then the money will follow. What I have been careful about is the amount of contracts I have.

It would be easy to pick up 30 deals a year and earn an extraordinary amount of money. It would be easy also to have to retire prematurely, having burnt myself out. I've seen this happen to others. A guy wins a major and his management encourages him to chase the dollar. All goes well for a year or two and then suddenly his results go down the pan, he stops winning, the publicity dries up and he wakes up one morning and stares at the face of a stranger as he is shaving. This is not my plan. I want to go on for at least another 10 or 15 years and to enjoy myself as well.

While my relationship with I M G and John Simpson is first class I insist that John tells me about everything. If a company proposes something and John doesn't feel it is right I still want to know about it. I might feel differently. Some critics say that managers push their clients too hard because they are on a percentage of earnings, which might be right. In the end those clients, like me, can say yes or no to any deal. The proposal might be a manager's, but the decision is mine. And mine alone. It is, after all, my life.

The same critics often attack appearance money as an evil within the game. Top players are promoted as villains, holding sponsors to ransom and insisting on large financial guarantees for them to turn up to play. I believe this is nonsense. It is not, however, a charge I wish to duck. The fact is that appearance money was around for a long time before I made any sort of mark on the golf scene. It was not my invention. Or Sandy's, or Seve's, or Nick's.

The truth, I suspect, is that appearance money of one sort or another has been paid for a very long time. Why else would a big-name player choose to travel many thousands of miles from his home to play in an event where the first prize is often less than the money he could receive for performing in an exhibition match? Of course, this does not apply to the really big tournaments and certainly not to the majors.

It is the sponsors themselves who decide which stars they want for their tournament and it is they who pay the asking price. Nobody is forced to do it. After all, golf is the only sport where even top performers begin each week's competition knowing that they could miss the cut and end up out of pocket. Nobody is paying us a weekly wage. We are, for the most part, out there hustling on our own.

From the sponsor's point of view there are obvious advantages to the system. The sponsor is guaranteed star names and this in turn helps create and sustain publicity for the event. Let me give an example. In 1985 I went to play in Australia. Along with David Graham, I was paid appearance money and this upset some local professionals who claimed we were taking money out of their tour which could and should be used as prize money.

Yet the facts were different. The sponsors were anxious to get television coverage but they were told by

Top left: My role-model. Gary Player in typical mood as he wins the 1978 US Masters, his third victory at Augusta

Top right: Four eyes should be better than two. Caddy Peter Coleman and I line up a crucial putt during the 1985 World Matchplay Championship at Wentworth

Above: Being introduced to the crowd before the 1985 Ryder Cup. Sam Torrance is left, Sandy Lyle right

Top left: Losing to Ballesteros at the 1985 World Matchplay. Seve's brother Vicente is in the middle

Top right: Old friend and foe Larry Nelson agrees to a half at the 18th during the 1987 Ryder Cup. It meant Europe could not lose the trophy we had won two years before

Above: With coaches Willi Hoffman (*left*) and Peter Kostis at Augusta 1986. I had every putter out of the shop at Augusta, but ended up with the one I brought with me

OPPOSITE

Above: Not an American in sight as I celebrate a putt holed during the 1985 Ryder Cup

Below: Ryder Cup joy. Ballesteros, myself, skipper Jacklin and Paul Way applaud Sam Torrance's approach shot to the last green as Europe beats the USA in the 1985 Ryder Cup match at The Belfry

The 1987 Ryder Cup: I chip in from a very difficult position between two bunkers at the 10th hole during the second day four-balls. The ball goes straight into the hole – one of the finest shots of my life

OPPOSITE

Working together with Sandy Lyle during the 1987 Ryder Cup at Muirfield Village, Ohio

Top: My coach Willi Hoffman shows how to dress for a British summer during the 1985 Open Championship at Royal St George's

Above: I overcame my back problems to win the 1988 Epson Matchplay Championship at St Pierre, Chepstow

OPPOSITE

Top left: A jubilant Sandy Lyle after winning the 1988 US Masters

Top right: Ian Woosnam battling against the rain on his way to victory in the 1988 PGA

Bottom left: Nick Faldo on the 18th green at the 1987 British Open

Bottom right: Blonds have more fun – with Australia's Greg Norman

The woman behind the man. Vikki lends her support at the 1985 Ryder Cup

the television company that without any stars they would have to pay 100,000 dollars for the privilege. So they engaged myself and Graham for considerably less than 100,000 dollars and got television. Without us, or some other stars, there might not have been a tournament for the local players to compete in and yet they openly criticized us and caused a public row without knowing the full facts.

Similarly, there are those who seem to think that appearance money is paid only in Europe, that in America the stars turn up every week like good little boys. It is true that appearance money is banned on the U S Tour but this does not mean it is not paid. I have heard of players being paid many thousands of dollars to redesign the putting green at the club where a tournament is being played. Others suddenly feature in a series of adverts or TV commercials for the company sponsoring a tournament. It is a way round the rule and it works but don't try telling me that there is no appearance money in the States.

My own first experience of appearance money came in 1980. I was invited to a tournament in Brazil where the first prize was 8000 dollars. It meant that even if I had been lucky enough to win I would just about have broken even. So I was offered a free flight and a free hotel booking, to cut my expenses. It was a simple and, to me, logical equation. The promoters wanted me to play but I wanted to earn money.

Since then there have been many invitations to many tournaments. Always I am consistent in what I request. I do not barter with anyone and I certainly do not ask for more from one guy and less from another. That would be unfair and, anyway, word would soon get around. I neither know, nor care, what anyone is getting. If Seve gets more, fine. If he gets less, fine. The only person I am concerned about in these matters is myself. I work out with IMG what is fair for me and then I stick to it. It's as simple as that.

The money also makes no difference to how hard I try to win a tournament. Trying to be the best is in my blood and I believe it is the same with the rest of the guys. I know there may have been some Americans in the early days who came to Europe and treated it as a bit of a holiday with appearance money thrown in but there have not been many like this. The vast majority of big-league players are too professional – and too proud – to do anything other than their best all the time.

Yet I am not naïve. I realize that the enormous amounts of money involved today can cause great envy. Certainly even I have been impressed when I read 'guesstimates' in the Press about my annual income. I have been less impressed, however, when I have looked at my bank balance for in order to put one dollar, one pound or one mark into my account, I must earn four or five times as much. The tax people take most of my earnings – they really are in the all-time winners' list – and I have large expenses. I employ my brother and another guy to help look after my business interests in Germany; IMG take a percentage and I have two homes to maintain on either side of the Atlantic. It means that, while I am doing okay, I could not contemplate retirement unless I was willing to live in a much more modest fashion than I have got used to over the last several years.

This is one of the reasons why I have set up my own golf course design company in partnership with IMG and architect Gerry Buckley who is not only one of the best but one of the most experienced course architects in the world. It is one of the most exciting projects I have ever entered into. I don't suppose there are many golfers – pro or amateur – who have not at some time designed a hole if only in their daydreams.

Now I have the chance to put some of my ideas into practice. It is fantastic to go to look over a piece of land and begin to imagine how it can be turned into a good course. It is also daunting but then I have found that if something is not challenging, then it is not really worth doing. I've played an awful lot of courses around the world, courses of every type imaginable, and while playing many of them I have thought that with just a little more thought that they could be improved.

We set up the company in October 1986 and by spring of 1987 we were in business. My first brand new course is just outside Paris. Meanwhile I am changing several courses in Germany, including Stuttgart, where my own tournament – the German Masters – is now staged each year. Soon I am hoping to begin work on new courses in Italy and in Spain, although my dream is to build a super course in Germany which has really fast, good greens as so far we cannot boast a course with great greens. The excuse is the weather but I do not accept this and, one day, I am determined to prove a lot of people wrong in Germany.

My own philosophy of design is simple enough. First, and most important, the course must be playable and enjoyable from the amateur point of view. It is the amateur, after all, who will be playing it most days. If the client wants a championship course then it is comparatively easy to design it so that it can be turned into a tough test for the professionals. There is no real point, however, in building a course that is *only* playable by the pros. Golfers want to enjoy themselves – not be humiliated every time they go out to play.

Hopefully one day I will realize my ambition of building a really fine course in Germany. Certainly golf has grown enormously in popularity over the last eight years and my own success has helped this growth at least a little. At the beginning of the eighties, for

example, there was no golf on television. Now each of the four majors is shown, plus the German Open and the German Masters and, usually, the World Series and the World Matchplay. What kids see they copy and so the future should be good for the game in my homeland.

Each year the number of German golfers increases by 10 to 15 per cent and this means increasing pressure on existing courses. It is a problem that must be solved if the sport is to truly thrive. Even the most enthusiastic of beginners can be discouraged if he or she cannot find somewhere to play or to practise. And yet old attitudes die hard. For example, I wanted to build a public driving range in Munich's Olympic Park where there is lots of land. I wrote to the mayor but I got a very negative response from him. He simply wasn't interested. I was surprised and disappointed.

Perhaps this official reluctance to acknowledge that golf is of some importance explains, in part, why no other German player has emerged since I made my own breakthrough. I thought one or two had a genuine chance to do so but thus far I'm on my own. I really hope this will be put right soon. I am aware of my responsibility to the game and to its future in Germany, but it would be nice to have another German on the Tour.

9

Other players and personal heroes

Every sportsman - and woman - has drawn inspiration from great players. Someone needs to set a record before it can be broken. Someone needs to establish the standard before it can be improved. And someone must have blazed a trail before a new generation of players even tries to extend the boundaries. When he was growing up, Bernhard Langer had no golfing heroes. This was not because there was no one who appealed to him, rather it was because information on the game was not readily available in a Germany consumed by soccer and a few other sports. As a teenager, however, Langer filled in some of the long hours of boredom as an assistant pro by reading about the game's history. English and American golf magazines found their way into his hands – and his were usually about the tenth hands to hold them – and slowly the heroes emerged. He is not an instinctive fan. Langer prefers to be a doer rather than a watcher but he appreciates excellence in others and, in particular, he relishes sportsmen who consult no compasses but who head off in their own direction, instinctively trusting their own judgement. Great champions must carry within them some real arrogance but Langer prefers this arrogance, this self-belief, to be kept to a reasonable level. Just because you are a great golfer does not mean you are a great human being. Or even a nice one. The sportsperson who begins to believe his or her own publicity is swiftly set aside by this modest German. When we talked about the players he admired he quickly pointed out that there were many heroes in life and that most of them went virtually unnoticed. Langer, to his credit, has a genuine grasp of reality. But, like the rest of us, he is not above talking enthusiastically about the golfers who have impressed him most – and the ordinary people who have played a significant part in his life.

Gary Player was always my idol. I just love the way he approaches golf. His attitude is exactly right. It is easy for me to identify with him because we are a similar size. Neither of us is the biggest guy in town. We also have similar, flat swings. It's a funny thing but there are fashions in golf swings just as there are fashions in clothes. At one time the Americans believed the upright swing was best but now most players try for a flat swing. Gary always had this sort of swing, as I did, because of his size.

He has also always stressed the importance of physical fitness and of eating properly. It is a credo I follow myself. Golf might not seem to make extraordinary physical demands but it can be very tiring playing 18 holes of high-pressure golf and it is obvious that the fitter you are then the easier it will be to maintain concentration. I had heard all about Gary long before I met him in 1976. I'd just pre-qualified for the British Open at Royal Birkdale and one day in the locker room Gary asked if I wanted to join him for a practice round. Want to? I was thrilled.

He could not have been kinder to me that day, passing on advice and tips all the time about the course, the way to approach an Open and how to best hit this shot or that one. It was also a lesson for me to see how hard he worked at his own game. Here he was, an established star, and yet he never stopped searching for a new way to hit the ball. I think of Gary Player and I think of practice. I also think of a very nice and kind man. A real hero.

No one will be surprised to learn that I admire Jack Nicklaus. Is there anyone who doesn't? Nicklaus is a great gentleman and a great ambassador for his country and his sport. He seems to have been at the top for ever now but the truth is that Nicklaus has had to overcome some tough times. He wasn't always the good-looking guy he is today. When he first emerged he was overweight and unpopular because he kept beating Arnold Palmer who was every American's hero at the time. It took a tough personality to live through those days when the gallery was baiting him and I admire Jack Nicklaus for the way he did it.

The other guy I admire is Palmer himself. I wasn't old enough to have seen Palmer at the height of his powers but I have watched the old films and even now the raw power of the man explodes right out of the screen. At his best, he was an unstoppable force – a bit like Seve can be at times. He has done more for pro golf and the modern game than anyone else. Our image is his image. Or should be.

The nice thing is that Arnold Palmer is also a gentleman. Now this might sound a little repetitious but the fact is that I have not met a so-called superstar who did not impress me as a basically decent guy. Maybe it's because they have proved what they set out to prove. Maybe it's because they are people of stature.

There is one golfer who, I believe, has the potential to be greater than any of them. Unfortunately for any golf managers who read this I have to admit that this player does not actually exist - except in my imagination. It is a game I play when I'm sitting at another airport, waiting for another plane to go to another tournament. So here, for the first time, is the perfect golfer - in my opinion anyway.

This mythical creature would drive like Greg Norman, hit fairway woods like Tom Kite, long irons (1-3) like Jack Nicklaus, medium irons after the fashion of Payne Stewart and have Ian Woosnam's accuracy with short irons. He would play out of bunkers like Tom Watson, pitch and chip like Seve and hole putts like Ben Crenshaw. So much for the technique of my creature. I also have to give him a head and a heart. No problem. I'll borrow both organs from Jack Nicklaus for there has never been a better thinker on the course or a more competitive player when it comes to actually winning. Now how much do you think this guy would make in a year?

There are, I'm happy to report, a few guys on the European Tour who would give such a mythical and redoubtable creature a run for his money. Seve, naturally, and I think I might give this 'Frankenstein creation' some trouble myself. Then there are a few British players who would be able to step inside the ropes and compete with my fantasy, and surely perfect, golfer.

Britain has always been one of the strongest

countries in the golf world. It is logically so. After all, most experts agree that the game was invented in Scotland - no matter what the Dutch claim - and it swiftly spread south, appealing to that uniquely British characteristic that demands a game to be played whenever more than one of them is gathered together.

For a time, however, it seemed as though the British stars were destined to be bit players when it came to the world stage. Through the sixties and much of the seventies - Tony Jacklin apart - there were few British guys who managed to really reach out and touch the heights when the world's great championships beckoned.

Indeed after Jacko's superb double triumph in the British and US Opens in 1969 and 1970, the long-suffering British public had their patience severely tested as they waited for the next genuine superstar to emerge. There were sound players on the scene, men like Peter Oosterhuis and Tommy Horton, Brian Barnes and Brian Hugget but few of them lived up to a critical public's expectations.

Part of the problem, I'm sure, has been what I used to experience myself. This is the fact that for most European golfers, the only major title available to them each season is the British Open. Qualification for the US Masters, the US Open and the USPGA are now beginning to slowly open out but until the last year or so, the Open appeared on each golfer's calendar like an invitation to the Holy Grail itself.

For weeks beforehand, the British media built up the event, concentrating naturally on those home-based players who stood a justifiable chance of actually winning the old claret jug. The players themselves began to think of little else, concentrating all their efforts into preparation for what is undoubtedly the most important week in the golfing calendar.

It meant that an already highly pressurised occasion was hyped up into a sort of modern-day trial by ordeal. No wonder – to me anyway – that so many outstanding British talents collapsed when the actual championship began. Their own expectations, and those of the British public, were simply too much for one man to bear. When it came to that critical moment, as it always does, in a great championship when a player *must* hold his game together under the most exquisite and nerve-wracking pressure, their games began to warp at the edges.

It is still a problem for many terrific British golfers. Despite the improvement in the number of invitations that the bigger European stars receive to play in the American majors, there are still not enough and many players only have the British Open as a recognisable and viable goal when each new season begins.

To me, it is no surprise that Sandy Lyle became the Briton who broke the apparent hoodoo that had hung over the Open for British players since Jacklin's great win at Royal Lytham St Annes. For a start, Sandy had been learning how to cope with major pressure for several years ever since he almost catapulted himself on to the European Tour in the late seventies.

The value of this learning process cannot be over-emphasized. We all must go through it. Before you can learn how to win, you have to experience how to lose and to educate yourself as a golfer each time you go through this painful experience. Sandy, thankfully, has been allowed to master his craft in America and beyond, away from the microscopic gaze of British TV and media. By the time he came to Royal St George's in 1985 he was ready. And it showed.

Statistically, Sandy Lyle can lay claim to being Number One without the need for any false modesty. Actually, in his case, such modesty would not be false at all because he is one of the least arrogant world-class sports personalities anyone could hope to meet. It is not that he does not have a precise appreciation of his talent or his worth in the game, it is just that his nature allows him to take these things in his stride and to put all his success into perspective.

Yet he remains a truly prodigious talent. In his first year on tour, 1978, he started quietly. Quietly? In fact he finished 49th which is not bad for a 20-year-old finding his feet in an alien environment. Since then he has only once finished outside the top 12 in Europe, when he finished the 1986 season in 'lowly' 24th spot. To do that he won £110,990 and this figure provides an interesting contrast with his second year on tour when he picked up £49,233 to become Europe's number one. How the times – and the money – have changed in so short a span.

So far Sandy has been top money winner in Europe on three separate occasions, 1979, 1980 and 1985. In the last three years he has won the Open and the US Masters to become the only golfer to win more than one major title in the last four seasons. He has also won the so-called Tournament Players' Championship in America and enjoyed victory in Japan.

In Europe alone he has broken through the million pound winnings barrier in just 10 years. It is, by any standards, a phenomenal record, one that allows him to be put forward as the best in the world in 1988, never mind top Briton. It impresses me even more when I think about how swiftly he found success and yet how he has maintained his appetite and, in recent years, sharpened it.

His advantages are obvious. The accident of birth that set him down on earth as the son of a professional golfer and that gave him a golf course as his own personal playground are obvious. Yet others have had the same sort of start and failed to make the mark.

The difference when it comes to Lyle is that Sandy has a remarkable gift that he has polished to shining brilliance over the last 30 years. He is so long off the tee that it can be embarrassing when he pulls out his driver and really gives it a rip. Often, thankfully, for the rest of us, he prefers a three wood or his one iron which he hits as far as we hit our drivers but which he likes because of the accuracy these clubs virtually guarantee him.

Arnold Palmer once chastised Sandy for not using his gift of length and sticking to his driver all the time. It is our luck that he has stuck to his guns and done it his way and after his recent successes who would dare argue that his is not the right way. For him at least. His natural temperament might well have been forged in the heat of battle and designed specifically for golf because he is almost totally unflappable. I like to think we are similar in this respect. And when his putting is on song then Sandy is capable of any score and of taking any title. He really could emerge as *the* outstanding golfer in the world over the next couple of years.

Or the man to emerge, as I've already suggested, could be Nick Faldo. Nick is a terribly strong character, a man whose own self-belief is almost unshakeable. You only have to look at the way he completely rebuilt his golf swing over a period of two years to know how strong he is.

When, in 1983, he won five European tournaments – including a unique hat-trick of wins – he single-handedly dominated the scene on this side of the Atlantic. His tall, good looks were reflected in a swing that looked aesthetically perfect. Then, after a mediocre couple of seasons in 1983 and 1985, Faldo suddenly took himself off to Florida to rebuild this swing. Most people had seen only beauty but he had detected an ugly flaw.

Despite all those wins Faldo alone realized that in the

pressure-cooker atmosphere of major championships he could play himself into contention – as he did at the Open and in the U S Masters – but that once there his normally reliable swing began to fray at vital moments. And Faldo wanted to taste major glory more than anything else.

It was the most difficult decision of his career to dismantle his swing. Most, if not all, of us at professional level know what our faults are and for us it is a constant fight to smooth them out, to readjust key points. I have even thought myself of completely restructuring my swing but, to be honest, I haven't got the courage for such a move. No one – and I don't care who it is who is advising a player – can reliably predict when such a swing rebuilding exercise will pay dividends. It might be months or it could be years. It might even be that the new swing does not work as well as the old one and that you never get the old one back into action again.

The odds, for me, are too high for such a gamble. I have decided to live with what I have. This is why I admire Nick's decision so much and why I say it demonstrates his single-mindedness and his determination to do things his way. There must have been many times when he felt like listening to all his critics who suggested, first in a whisper and then in a roar, that he was quite simply mad.

Suddenly the confident man who was beginning to stride around the world's fairways with genuine purpose looked unsettled, uncomfortable and out of touch with himself. His results went backwards, his name slowly began to slide out of the newspapers and his face to disappear off the TV screens. Many saw it as a form of professional suicide.

Yet through all this nightmare that lasted the best part of two years, Nick, to my knowledge, never really faltered once. He stressed to everyone who asked that he knew what he was doing and, more importantly, he knew what he was aiming for. The target was in front of him and he willed himself to score a direct hit.

In the end we know that it paid off for him. He believes that his victory in the 1987 Open Championship was due entirely to the work he had put in over the previous 24 months, and who am I to argue with his theory? The fact is that he did stand up to all the pressure thrown at him at Turnberry and his last round of 18 straight pars is eloquent testimony to that fact.

So suddenly, after such a barren spell, Britain had two Open champions in the space of 24 months. It was no accident that the two heroes were Lyle and Faldo, two young men who had been rivals over the years since they had first met as schoolboy competitors. Their rivalry had sharpened them up for the battles to come and although they are friends, it was as important as anything else in helping to forge them into great champions.

Now there is another potential champion in Britain. After the Scot and the Englishman, enter the Welsh-man. The Welsh, I believe, are a race famed for their battling qualities, their refusal to give in unless unconscious and most likely tied up as well. Defeat is not a word recognized in the Welsh language. Instead they have a word called 'hwyl'. I'm not sure exactly what it means in translation but I understand it is something like spirit, a never-say-die attitude that has been perfectly encompassed by little Ian Woosnam.

I'm not the biggest guy in the world of golf so I hope Ian forgives me if I draw attention to his size. He says he is 5 feet 4½ inches but so far he has refused to stand still long enough for any of us to get a tape measure to check out this fact. When he stands on the tee, however, Ian Woosnam is nine feet tall. I don't know anyone who hits the ball harder or straighter when he is in form.

His swing is very simple and very effective. First, though, he had to struggle on the tour. Yet while he was suffering from lack of money and the problems that this curse brings, he never once thought of packing it up. His confidence never wavered and if you made the mistake of standing still long enough, Ian would invariably tell you how one day he was going to be a winner. It was, I suppose, the old 'hwyl' bubbling to the surface.

Well, he certainly proved it last year when he had one of the most remarkable seasons of all time. He finished the season with record winnings in Europe of £439,075, for the number one spot. Worldwide he won well over one million pounds – the first golfer so to do – and he added the World Matchplay Championship, a first for Britain, *and* the World Cup for Wales just for good measure. It was truly astonishing stuff and we all delighted in his success for there is no more attractive a personality or bubbly a character on the European scene.

But if this trio represents the current pinnacle of success from the British players, there are others who I believe should have made it in a big way and yet haven't, players who have flattered to deceive, candles that have first blown in the wind and then been snuffed out by it.

Such a player, for example, is Bill Longmuir. I played against Bill in the 1988 Epson Matchplay and I had a very hard game, winning over extra holes at St Pierre.

As I played that match I couldn't help but wonder why he has not been a much more significant figure in Europe and, indeed, the world. Ever since he first emerged with a record-breaking round during the 1979 British Open, I have been expecting Longmuir to break free of the rank and file who make up the professional circus. Now I fear it may be too late and for the life of me I cannot understand it.

Longmuir's swing has always impressed me, his

attitude is good, and yet he never quite makes it. I do not mean this unkindly and I have just chosen Bill as an example, for there are others who have suffered a similar fate. Maybe it just illustrates how thin the dividing line is between outstanding success and relative failure. I say relative for Bill Longmuir has had his successes, notably in Africa, but never in Europe.

I would have thought, for example, that the all-exempt tour would have suited Longmuir and others who have been around for quite a long time without quite managing to make the breakthrough. In the 'bad old days' many players had to pre-qualify for a tournament so that by the time they came to the competition proper their nerve-ends were already beginning to show signs of wear and tear.

Then they had to concentrate on making the halfway cut, perhaps pick up a few hundred pounds and so qualify automatically for the following week. It was a hard school; in many ways too hard and it encouraged defensive golf from the majority of players while the guys good enough to make the top layer in Europe were virtually out on their own and playing in a separate tournament, the one that determined who actually won.

Now it has all changed and we are beginning to see the true consequences of such a radical restructuring of the system. It is why – at least in my belief it is why – we are suddenly seeing new names not just on the leader boards but on the winner's cheque as well in 1988. The overall attitude has changed drastically. These days the guys go out with the intention of 'giving it a go'. If they fail there is always the certainty of another chance the following week. The old doubts have gone and in their place we now see renewed confidence from players perfectly capable of upsetting the big-name players and digging out their own bit of glory.

It has happened already in the States and I'm glad to

see it beginning to happen in Europe because it is a much healthier state of affairs.

Thinking about personal heroes, however, I cannot leave this section without paying tribute to three men who have helped me achieve success. Two of them are German, Heinz Fehring and Willi Hoffman, while the third is my caddy, Peter Coleman. Life is similar to a jigsaw puzzle. At the beginning there are many blank spaces which need to be filled but how these spaces are filled depends on the people we each meet. I have been very lucky.

Heinz was to me what Professor Higgins was to Eliza. When I left Anhausen for Munich I was a really raw teenager, a 14-year-old filled with enthusiasm but with little knowledge of the world and almost totally lacking in any kind of sophistication. Heinz not only began to work on improving my swing, he worked hard on improving me as a person. He taught me how to dress correctly, how to hold my own in social circumstances, how to look after myself.

Gradually, under his coaching, the shy and awkward young man who had arrived at Munich began to feel more comfortable and less tongue-tied. Heinz, in those days, was like a second father to me, a man I could rely on and a person who always had time to listen to my problems. I shall be eternally grateful to him.

Heinz and I have remained very close friends but as my career took me away from Germany and on to the international sporting treadmill I turned more and more to Willi Hoffman for help with my game. While Heinz was committed to Munich, Willi was more flexible and it was more convenient to see him when I had a swing problem. He started as a coach and has become another close and much-appreciated friend.

Over the years, Willi has been a great supporter for me. He has spent many hours working with me and has been very careful in the way he has handled me. Any changes he has made, he has made gradually so that I have been able to assimilate them properly.

Whenever I need his help he always seems to have the time to see me. Nowadays, I usually see him between five and eight weeks a year to work on my swing, usually built around the major titles. Together we run a series of golf schools in conjunction with the Club Corporation of Europe in Germany and we have put together a manual on how the golf swing should be taught. Pupils at the schools receive lessons from Willi and some other coaches and I do a series of clinics.

My caddy, Peter Coleman, first approached me in 1981 to suggest we work together. Even by then I knew his reputation as one of the best caddies on the tour. Peter was good enough as a player to have been an assistant professional and so he knows quite a lot about the mechanics of the swing and what it takes to win under pressure.

Right from the start we got on together very well. Like me, he is very professional. He always looks right, dresses correctly and believes it is important not just to be clean and tidy but to be punctual. I cannot recall Peter ever being late. I trust him absolutely over things like yardages and always discuss club selection with him. It is as a team that we operate. Of course, he has made mistakes sometimes; but when you are making 40 to 50 decisions each day then there are bound to be errors - with Peter there are not many.

Because I like to work hard, to practice regularly and to stay on the putting green for many long hours, it is important that I have a caddy who is prepared to work alongside me. Peter has never complained. He knows that the harder I work, the better I will play and the more money he will earn. It is a mutually advantageous deal. Yet after our partnership began in 1981, Peter left me to work with Greg Norman for a time in 1982 and 1983. The reason was simple: I was not earning enough prize money for Peter to make a decent living himself.

Although I was naturally disappointed, I could understand his point and I appreciated his honesty in telling me quickly that he just had to go to someone else to earn his daily bread. In 1983, however, he returned to work for me and we have been a regular partnership ever since, sharing many great memories over the last few years.

He is naturally a very positive person and a man whose nature matches my own. I like to remain calm and Peter is the same. When it comes down to the last few holes in a tournament – or 'the clutch' as we know it on the tour – then Peter does not get over-excited or nervous. He remains very cool, very professional and extremely supportive. This is vital because there are times when, like everyone else, I get down. Sometimes when I have made a few bogeys in a row I feel as though I'll never get another birdie in my life. It is then that Peter helps to lift my spirits.

If I fail to win a title after being strongly in contention then he never complains. Instead he says 'don't worry, we will do better next time'. Some caddies make their displeasure at missing out on a fat pay cheque very obvious but Peter has never been like that. He knows that I have always tried my best and that has always been good enough for him.

After my great year in 1985, Peter celebrated by treating himself to a Porsche. It made a lot of headlines at the time and I was very pleased for him. We all have our dreams and Peter was able to achieve one of his when he bought his car. It was a purchase that also helped to upgrade the status of the caddy on the tour. Like several others, Peter is one of a new breed of caddies: intelligent people who act and look professional and who are an integral part of the golf scene. At one time caddies were treated as second-class citizens but I am happy to go anywhere, dine any time, with Peter and, hopefully, there are many celebration dinners ahead of us both.

Whenever these celebrations take place, I always remember the people who have helped me carve out my career. There are so many of them, too numerous to mention really. People like Frau Van Eyck, a member at Munich Golf Club, and the lady who helped teach me English and who befriended me when I was a young assistant. And then there is Jens Schnieders, a golf fan who helped me financially to survive the early days on the tour and who asked for nothing in return except that I try my best. I am grateful to them all.

10

Winning some – losing more!

Through most of the eighties Bernhard Langer has been enjoying a roller-coaster ride through golf. In 1981 and 1982 he made his reputation, emerging from the pack to prove himself a winner and a golfer of genuine commitment. Since he won the Dunlop Masters in 1980 Langer has picked up – to date – 18 more titles on the European Tour. Only Seve Ballesteros has exceeded this total of 19 victories but Langer has, arguably, been a little more consistent. His nature is so unflappable, his approach so meticulous that he is a contender every time he tees up the ball. And when he is on his game then there is no one in the world who can live with him.

The great Jack Nicklaus has gone on record as saying that golf, unlike any other sport, is a game in which if you are successful just 20 per cent of the time then you are the best in the world. One of the basic secrets of this success, therefore, is accepting that at least 80 per cent of the time you play, you will fail. It is a criteria that - if applied to tennis or athletics, soccer or even skiing - would have coaches and managers rushing to the nearest psychiatrist. Yet if this 'Holy Grail' notion of golf is analyzed it is easy to see that Nicklaus is right. Even at the height of his prodigious talent Nicklaus lost far more events than he won and he is reckoned to have been the greatest golfer ever to lift a club.

This need to accept defeat and to learn how to live with the vagaries of weather and luck, the bounce of the ball and the sometimes ridiculous good fortune of opponents is both golf's curse and its blessing. It means that no tournament is ever cut and dried before the last putt has dropped. There is, it is true, a certain circus-like routine to the major tours but there is not much repetition to the list of winners. Unlike tennis - and tennis is the nearest comparison in tour terms - the same names do not crop up each week. By its very nature, golf not only creates sporting gods, it also constantly reminds them that they are only human and that there are many more where they came from...

Winning golf tournaments is never easy. Too many things can go wrong too often for that to be the case. I've discovered, however, like other good players before me that doing well in pro golf can become a habit. The trick is to make the breakthrough, for the hardest tournament of all to win is the first. Once that landmark has been achieved then a player's confidence increases, self-belief soars. It is an ordeal by fire that everyone who harbours hopes of becoming a top-class professional must endure. But at the end of that great day there is no prouder sportsperson in the world than the golfer who has just lifted his or her first significant title.

My breakthrough in the Dunlop Masters in 1980 was particularly satisfying. Some critics might say that because the Dunlop event was invitational that there was not the depth of opposition that can be found in normal tournaments where anything up to 150 golfers tee it up. In fact, the reverse is true. Because it is invitational and because the money was so good in those days I knew that Sunday night in Chepstow that I had just beaten 50 of the best players around. My sense of satisfaction was heightened.

As usual I did not immediately hurtle off into some wild celebration. I'm happy to buy other people a drink but I do not enjoy alcohol myself and while I was happy that night I did not need to do anything silly to show the world that I felt as though I was in orbit around the moon. This is just the way I am. Most days I feel pretty much the same. I don't suffer the black moods that other people seem to get but then I don't feel the need to jump on a table and tell everyone how good I feel now and then either. I'm basically a contented and fairly placid person. Some critics may feel this makes me a little bland but it is only the way one perceives it. Certainly I can assure you that I am not Mr Spock's cousin, that I have plenty of feelings and emotions and do not mind showing them. It is just a question of where and when. The man you see at work on a golf course is a professional sportsman trying to rein in his emotions, to concentrate wholly on the task facing him.

As far as I am concerned there is a time to work and a time to play. Alright, in my case it seems to be all play but golf at the top is a serious business. You can never merely 'make it' and then coast. If you do that then there is only one direction in which to coast and that is downhill. If anything, I've found that achieving success is far from being an end in itself, that I have to work and to concentrate harder than ever these days. I don't mind that at all. It is simply what I have to do but it is hard to please all of the people all of the time. All I try to do is please myself and my family and hope that the rest will follow.

I admire someone like Lee Trevino who can make it all seem so easy, so effortless at times and who can amuse the gallery. But Lee is a natural comedian, an intuitively funny man. Yet even in his case he needs time on his own, space away from the crowds who demand his attention. When he finishes his day's play, then Lee will head off to his own hotel room where he likes to eat privately – as we all do at times. The fact is that the public expect him to be amusing all the time so that it has become increasingly difficult for him to discard the patter and the jokes and just be an ordinary guy.

For myself, I enjoy dining with others and having a few laughs to help ease away the tension of the day. I like the company of other people. I'm not a joke-teller but I enjoy hearing an amusing tale told by someone who has such a gift. Life must not be taken seriously all the time.

Certainly, there was no problem laughing on that Sunday night after I had won the Dunlop Masters. And after laughing I then prayed to God to thank him for my success. Not because I thought He had singled me out for special treatment but because through Him I had been allowed to express myself and to enjoy a tangible reward after a lot of very hard work.

No sooner had I finished praying, however, than the full impact of what I had achieved hit me. Suddenly I realized that winning this first big title merely meant that the spotlight would be on me for a while, that now the target had to be to win again quickly. Otherwise I would be labelled a one-win fluke, my own confidence would drop and the future would look less attractive. It is like climbing a large hill. The peak always seems to be just over the next ridge but in reality the peak is usually just as far away as ever.

I cannot explain properly why it is that I want to go on. Sure, there are many things yet to achieve, many goals to set myself but this in itself is not a rational explanation of my urge to take my talent to the limit. I could throttle back, I could lie in the sun more, spend more time with my family and yet I choose to continue to work and to travel to foreign lands.

Yet, while I find it difficult to come up with the correct words to describe my own desire to keep chasing some mythical and distant beast, I can recognize easily the same desire in others. Seve has it. So, too, did Jack Nicklaus and the same applies to Arnold Palmer, to Gary Player and to many others. I suppose it is the joy at finding something you do well, something that brings joy to oneself and enjoyment to others.

I feel God has given me this talent to be a good golfer and that He has chosen to send me around the globe playing the game and entertaining people. I shall continue to play golf for as long as He chooses. If I would like people to know anything then it is that it takes more than talent to be a success, it is a gift that only God can give us.

Yes, there are great rewards to be had from living my life. There is the thrill of combat, the comradeship of being in the middle of a group of men chasing the same target and suffering the same problems and, of course, the sheer excitement of competing at the top in the full glare of a baleful and sometimes critical public eye.

It is all these things - and more. It is basically indescribable but, equally, it cannot be shrugged off.

Nor do I want to toss ambition aside. I am still a young man and what could I find to replace the satisfaction golf brings me? As I've said before I try to keep it all in the right perspective and never forget where I come from and why I am here. We all must tread the path that stretches before us and mine is a road that leads always and inevitably to a golf course.

Eventually, one day this path will lead to my own golf course, to my special place. At present I am looking for the right piece of real estate in Germany upon which I can create my own course and on which ultimately my own tournament – the German Masters – will be staged. Like many before me, I dream of creating a super tournament, an event that will transcend the ordinary and become part of the game's mythology. High-blown ambitions maybe but everyone has to start with a dream.

It would give me great pleasure to prove that a great golf event can be staged in my own country where there is still so much to be learned about maintaining a course in top-class condition and preparing it for a professional event. Certainly I have learned a tremendous amount from helping to stage the German Masters. I have also learned to appreciate fully the time and the effort it takes for any event to be staged.

Perhaps too many of us too often turn up for an event, play in the pro-am, play in the competition proper and then depart without taking time out to consider and be thankful for the many weeks and months that have gone into getting this one course ready for us to earn our living.

Certainly, it is exquisitely difficult to get the course into the right condition. Take the fairways, for example. Most club golfers like a fair amount of grass on the fairways, they enjoy them lush because when it is like that, they get the feeling that they can easily swing the club underneath the ball. It is as much psychological as anything else but to them it is preferable. The professional player, however, likes exactly the opposite, preferring close-cut grass so the ball stands out on its own and so that he or she can then 'work' the ball better.

Then with my own tournament, there is the problem of coping fairly and satisfactorily with different sponsors. It is only too easy to be thought to be giving more to one sponsor than to another, although this has never been the case. It is a bit like trying to keep all your children happy and contented at one and the same time. Practically impossible but at least it means there is never a dull moment.

Plus there is the simple commercial aspect to the event which is run jointly between myself and I M G. On the one hand, we want to put on a really good show, to impress everyone and give the public a good time so that they want to return the following year. At the same time, it is a financial investment and we all hope to see some sort of return on our money. There is, however, no way to look for an instant profit.

Certainly, in the first few years I do not expect to make any cash, nor do I M G. It is the long-term return that is our goal and the establishing of a tournament that will carry with it prestige and a reputation for being done correctly. In the meantime, the best we can hope to do is to break even.

My first German Masters was staged at Stuttgart in 1987 and I was pleased with the way things went that week although I must confess to being very nervous about it all. Usually, if there are any complaints during a tournament from the public, the Press, TV or the players, I can either agree, disagree or simply ignore it. This time the complaints affected me personally because it was my tournament. My name was up front and I was there to be shot at by anyone and everyone.

Fortunately, it all went pretty smoothly. Sure, there were a few problems but it was our first year and no one can expect things to be perfect first time round. We can learn from our past mistakes and make next year's tournament even better. I was happy with the results from the first year and know the future will only be better.

Right from the start I insisted with my partners that the main priority had to be the players. Everything else had to fit in around their requirements. It is like putting on a play. If the stage is not the right size, if the lighting and sound systems are not first class then you can have the finest actors in the world performing and it will still be a shambles. I was determined this would not happen at Stuttgart.

So whatever I felt the players needed, I tried to provide and they then could concentrate wholly on what they do best... playing golf and entertaining the public. The course was priority one and I now realize just how much heartache, headache and backache goes into preparing a stretch of land so that, like an Olympic athlete in training, it peaks at exactly the right time. I tried to make it a test of skill but a fair test, not something that exposed players to public ridicule as somtimes happens when courses are tricked up too much.

Then I had to make sure that at least some of the biggest names were at the German Masters. The standard had to be set right from the start, the event had to be seen to be a big-time competition and the only way to ensure this was to pay the appropriate money. If you want the best then you have to pay for it. It is as simple as that. Anyway, as a player who has benefitted over the years from the appearance money system, I could hardly refuse to stick to the same method when it came to my own tournament.

In truth, a golf tournament is like some giant money-laden iceberg. All that ever gets mentioned is the prize fund but this is just the visible tip of the financial mountain that any company or entrepeneur must scale if they are to set up a successful week.

Prize money in Stuttgart, for example, was £300,000 in 1987 but the real cost of setting up this week was around £1,000,000. There is so much to be paid for and, unlike America, where each event has local and voluntary help, in Europe you must pay everyone from the person on the gate to the kids deployed to pick up the litter. It is an enormous financial outlay and one that no one can enter into lightly. At the same time it is an adventure and a challenge to me personally to try to arrange a terrific week from every point of view.

To be honest, I'm not yet sure whether or not I am a good businessman. Only time will tell. All I can do is set my standards high, deal directly and honestly and hope that everyone else does the same. Tournament weeks are improving all the time in Europe.

We struggle from time to time with things like practice facilities and the weather can frequently be a nuisance but the progress made in course maintenance and condition has been reflected in the steady improvement in scoring over the last decade. What we sow, we reap. In golf this is quite literally true and I am delighted that the current crop is of such high quality.

There is even evidence that other areas are being brought up to the standard set in America since the early sixties. We now have courtesy cars available at every tournament and though this does not seem very much, it is another minor problem off players' hands when they are beginning to concentrate on playing the best golf they can.

At the Epson Matchplay Championship - which I was delighted to win in 1988 - we even had a crèche for the players' children. They have had these crèches in the States for a long time but they are only just beginning to emerge in Europe, thanks to the hard work of sponsors and players' wives. More and more players now have the financial resources to enable them to bring along their families when they are competing. Most players are relatively young and so their children are usually at the baby or toddler stage. How much better it is for a hard-pressed young mum to be able to accompany her husband to a tournament week, to share more deeply in his professional life and to have a break from her own often lonely routine at home without him for long stretches of the year.

This sort of simple breakthrough means not only that marriages are more likely to survive the strain of constant separation but it means also that the players are happier, more content and so the sporting spin-off is that their golf game should reflect their improved state of mind. That, anyway, is the theory.

It is something we now hope to do for the German Masters, another little improvement. Meanwhile, we are off to a good start. What matters is that we had a great week and that the winner, Sandy Lyle, was exactly the sort of high-quality victor I had hoped to see emerge in this first tournament. Sandy's is a good name to have down on what I hope will be a long and glittering Roll of Honour from the German Masters.

And if nothing else, at least I'll come out of the experience of promoting this tournament with a world-class knowledge about how to really cut the grass. Mind you, it's an expensive way to learn such an apparently easy task.

11

Personally speaking...

Like many sportsmen before him, Bernhard Langer devoted most of his youth to the pursuit of excellence in his chosen game. It meant many long hours on the driving range, the putting green and on the course itself. It meant discipline when his mates and the usual sirens were wailing seductively from their discos and clubs. Langer hardly ever wavered. He was never a hermit, however, and always tried to weave into his life a normal existence alongside the friends he had known since he first toddled around to the house next door in Anhausen. He was helped by the severity of the German winters which meant that for a few months each year

*golf ceased to exist except in the imagination and it was
during these winter months that Langer lived like any
other teenager. Then when he went on the European
Tour his appetite for work stayed with him. He has
never been the sort of guy who finished a round and
then went in search of some watering hole. Dedication
had been his mistress – and still is.*

*His caddy for the last several years, Peter Coleman,
says he has never seen a top-class golfer who is willing
to work harder or longer on his game, that Bernhard is
in many ways the complete professional. And Coleman
should know. In his time, Peter has caddied for –
amongst others – Severiano Ballesteros and Greg
Norman, neither of whom shirk the hard work that top-
class golf demands. Even though golf had to be the
priority in Langer's life for a long time, there eventually
came a moment when he realized that he wanted
something else besides, that a future landscape filled
with no more than a succession of anonymous hotel
rooms was a very bleak landscape indeed. In other
words, by the time Langer reached his mid-twenties he
was ready to fall in love. Happily, this development
coincided with the arrival on the golf scene one day of
an air stewardess called Vikki. For both of them life was
never to be quite the same again...*

Fortunately I don't miss halfway cuts very often. When
I exited from the Dunhill British Masters in June 1988,
for example, it was the first time in 59 European
tournaments that I had failed to complete four rounds.
Before that event, one of the few cuts I did miss was
during the Inverrary Classic in Florida in March 1983.
After changing my shoes in the locker room, I headed
off with a German friend who was over in the States to
see if I could rustle up a courtesy car.

As we came out of the locker room, we saw two girls

standing outside obviously waiting for someone. We said, 'Hi, waiting for us?' just to draw their attention and they both laughed. But that was all and I carried on up some stairs to order the car. Then as we came back down we met the girls again. This time they were with one of the American players, Randy Cavanaugh, his caddy and some other guys.

We all stood there chatting for a while and then Randy asked us if we would like to join them all for dinner. Well, we had nothing else to do that evening except eat by ourselves and so we eagerly agreed. That evening over dinner I spent most of my time chatting to one of the girls, Vikki, and realized suddenly that I was really attracted to her. She was not just very pretty, she was interesting and amusing company. Before the bill had been paid I'd made another date with her.

It was the start of a real romance that spun through the next several weeks. Vikki was working as a stewardess with Eastern Airlines at the time and so she was able to take days off en bloc to coincide with where I was playing. She came up to Bay Hill to see me and then we spent almost three weeks seeing each other in the Florida area. Soon after, I had to return to Europe and that was when I learned just how expensive telephone bills can get as we continued our relationshp... only this time it was long distance and our chaperone was an operator.

We talked almost every day by phone but after a while I realized that just hearing her voice was only underlining how much I missed her. Suddenly I felt very lonely. I decided that we had to make up our minds about each other. We had to either take our relationship further or else finish it. Making hundreds of phone calls was no substitute for seeing each other. So I asked Vikki to take a few weeks off and to come over to Europe to see me. Fortunately, she had some holiday time owing and

she agreed to visit me. It was her first time outside
the United States and a really big decision for her to
make.

The three weeks that she spent with me that year were
among the happiest of my life. I took her to as many
places as I could but the time we spent in Paris lives in
my memory. It is a romantic city to start with but, even
though I'd been to Paris many times, showing this great
capital to her was like seeing it again for the first time
myself. Before the end of these magical three weeks I
knew that I was irreversibly in love with her.

We hadn't mentioned marriage during this period but
we both knew how we felt about each other. Before she
had to go back to the USA I took her to my home and
introduced her to my parents which went fine as they
took to her straight away. Then she had to leave and the
loneliness closed in around me like an unwanted cloak.
Four months after we first met I asked her to make the
biggest decision of her life; to quit her job and to be with
me. To my delight she agreed.

We then spent six weeks travelling together as I
played all over the world. It was a tough initiation for
Vikki into the sort of life the wives of the golfers must
endure. We took in the States, Australia, Europe and
Japan. It was a diet of constant travel and about as
tough and tiring as these things can be. She had to cope
not only with the travelling but with having to spend
many long hours on her own as I played or practised. It
was a challenge that would either make or break us as
far as the future was concerned.

Thankfully, she coped well and enjoyed the experience. I now knew for certain that this was the woman
with whom I wished to share my life and so I proposed.
In September we became engaged and set our marriage
date for 21 January 1984. Vikki's parents are no longer
alive sadly so she agreed to our getting married in
Anhausen in the church were I had once served as an

altar boy. In return I promised to help fly over some of her friends and relatives.

I had decided to take off five weeks prior to the wedding to help plan the occasion. It was the longest break away from golf I had enjoyed for several years. When the big day came it dawned cold and beautiful. The skies were cloudless blue and the 10 inches of snow that lay on the ground sparkled in the sunlight. It was perfect.

Although it was only a small wedding – we had about 100 guests – the event attracted a lot of media attention in Germany and lots of photographers turned up on the day. We asked them to wait outside the church as we wished to enjoy this ceremony privately and then we posed for as many pictures as they wanted and even built a snowman and his wife before heading off for our reception.

It was here that Vikki probably had the biggest surprise of her wedding day when the cake was brought in. She was expecting a cake with lots of white icing but this is not a German tradition and as we both loved chocolate I had ordered a dark chocolate cake which rather stunned my new bride. One tradition we do have, however, is that the bride is 'kidnapped' at some time during the reception, while the groom's back is turned. The game then is for the groom to find his wife before the day ends. This is not as easy as it sounds because the bride can be taken anywhere in the town.

Fortunately, Anhausen is only a small place and it took less than two hours before I found her with my brother and other friends. They had gone to a restaurant at a local tennis club and were happily smashed on champagne which, traditionally, I then had to pay for – so you can see there is an incentive to find the lady as quickly as possible. Before we left the tennis club we even played tennis together, both of us in our wedding finery.

Then it was back to the reception where we stayed until two o'clock in the morning before heading off to our apartment. There, strung outside for everyone to see, our friends had put up a clothes line with baby clothes and a stork swaying in the evening breeze. They had been busy inside the apartment too where they had littered the floors, the bed and every drawer with tiny, ripped-up pieces of newspaper. It was a mess but we didn't mind in the slightest. It may not have been the perfect end to the day but it had been a perfect day.

So I was married. The responsibility worried me just as it does every other young groom. I was now 26 and suddenly I had another person to consider always. If I missed a cut now it was not just me who had to take a paycut. This anxiety was not helped by the thought that sportsmen sometimes suffer a loss of form during the first year of their marriage.

In the event 1984 turned out to be a very good year for me. I finished the year number one in Europe for the second time after winning four tournaments - the French, Dutch, Irish and Spanish Opens - and I began to really find my way in America where I won over 80,000 dollars for 75th place on their money list after playing in only eight tournaments. Instead of holding me back, marriage had inspired me. I began to feel more content. Put it another way... Vikki equalled happiness which in turn helped my golf. Now there was another reason to try to win, to practise and to compete.

With Vikki's help I learned to relax more off the course and to begin to enjoy life more. I even relaxed my grip on the money I had earned. By this I don't mean I had ever been mean but I had been careful. After never having money as a child and a teenager I perhaps never quite believed that someone was not going to appear and take it all away from me. Now I'm happy to indulge my family. Compared to Greg Norman, I'm still not a big spender but compared to my old self I am a spendthrift.

Life since my marriage could hardly have been better. Vikki has never lost her enthusiasm for accompanying me to tournaments and we travel almost everywhere together. In a normal year I play around 35 events and Vikki - and now my daughter Jackie - will be with me for at least 32. It means that over the years we have had to become skilled in the sheer logistics of moving a family around. It is not easy because usually we carry with us half a dozen or more pieces of luggage so that we do not so much require courtesy cars as a courtesy truck.

Still, it is worth it. I am never happier than when I am with my family and, apart from seeing Vikki regularly, I have been determined to share in the joy of watching my daughter grow up. Jackie, actually, was conceived during a trip to Australia and born on 19 July 1986. Golf afficionados will realize instantly that this was the Saturday of the British Open at Turnberry. I regret very much not being present at the birth. Vikki had travelled with me right up until the last few weeks of her pregnancy and then she had gone to stay with my parents in Anhausen while I played.

If I had known the baby was due that Saturday then I might well have flown home. But Vikki entered into a nice conspiracy to keep the information from me as I was playing well and in contention for the Open title at the time. I did not realize she had gone into hospital until it was too late for me to do anything about it which was probably just as well really. It would have taken at least eight hours to get home from Scotland and by then I would have been too late to see the birth anyway. When the news came that I had a daughter I could hardly believe it. I may not have gone on to win the Open - too much can happen to one man in one weekend after all - but even that year's victor, my friend Greg

Norman, cannot have felt as much pleasure as I did that Saturday in Scotland.

As soon as I could after play finished I set off for home and my wife and new child. I remember vividly the first time I saw them together. My first concern, naturally, was for Vikki and then I turned to my daughter. She was impossibly perfect and beautiful. Until then I had always thought of babies as little, ugly things, sort of dried up like prunes but not this child. Probably every father feels the same but I was left with a great sense of awe when I held her in my arms. No golf trophy could ever possibly compete with the joy I felt right then; no title could supercede the sheer delight and wonder I sensed that I had helped created this perfect little human being.

And this is how it has been ever since. My whole life has taken on new shades thanks to Vikki and Jackie. No matter how well or how badly I have played they are waiting for me at the end of the day. If I come back to a hotel disappointed at my performance I do not have time to dwell on it. Instead my daughter lifts me into her world and the mundane concerns of playing golf recede rapidly into the background. Nowadays Jackie is a seasoned traveller herself. She began travelling when she was $2\frac{1}{2}$ weeks old and now she is an old hand at finding her way around different hotels and houses.

Right from the start I have tried my best to be a proper parent. I have always helped bathe her, change her nappy and generally involve myself in her life and in Vikki's. Parenthood, like life itself, is something we share between us. Between them, Vikki and Jackie provide a central point in my life. The same, to a lesser extent obviously, has been true of sport.

Golf is my game, my living and my first sporting love but I am, to be honest, a complete sports nut. For example, I love to ski and always leave at least one week a year free so that I can indulge my passion for sweeping down a mountain in as fast a time as I dare.

I have skiied ever since I was a small boy when, along with the other kids in Anhausen, I used to practise on the gentle hills around the village. I was 18 years old before I actually went on to proper mountains and the thrill of skiing ·.p there where eagles soar has never left me. And I am a good skier, probably two or three handicap. I like to go on black runs and off-piste although I always plan my trips so that if I am injured then there is time to recover before the crucial tournaments start in the spring. So far, however, I have not been injured at all.

The great thing about skiing is that once you have mastered the technique it stays with you always. I could stop skiing for three years and then pick it up again from where I left off. The same is not true of golf. If I did not play golf for three years then a 12-handicap player would stand a good chance of beating me off scratch when I went out on the course again.

My other main sporting passions are football and tennis. I have supported Bayern Munich all my life and try to see them play whenever possible. I still like to play soccer too, although the opportunities are limited these days. Sometimes my friend Franz Beckenbauer invites me to watch the German national side play and often we combine these trips with a few holes of golf. Franz is, as you might suspect, an elegant golfer. He plays the game like he did his football with grace and without apparent effort. It is a delight to have him as a friend now because he was one of my first sports heroes.

So far, however, one of Germany's other great sporting heroes, Boris Becker, has not asked me to have a game of tennis. This, I must admit, is a relief because I fear Boris would blow me off the court. Although I love tennis I cannot claim to be better than, say, 18 handicap at the game. I enjoy, however, playing tennis as much as possible. It is such an antidote to golf because in golf you have so much time to think whereas in tennis it is all reaction and so quick.

But whether it is skiing, tennis, football or my cycling or my card-playing, I always try my best, my hardest. Not to win necessarily but to compete, to be stretched. That, I believe, is the way to have most fun. I do not take my sporting hobbies seriously but I do try to seriously enjoy them. There is a difference.

12

Reflections on the future

Performing at the very top of the golf game holds a paradoxical situation for any player talented enough to inhabit this special world. On the one hand, he or she has to suffer endless demands on his time. On the other he or she faces exquisite boredom as they find themselves with long, yawning hours to fill as they wait for a round to begin or another plane to cross a stretch of ocean. Langer, more than most players, is equipped to cope with these twin demands. On long journeys, for example, he has developed the knack of switching his brain into neutral, of cruising along on automatic pilot. Professionally, he divides his day up according to what

*is expected of him and he never, ever, attempts to do
more than he knows he can handle. He is fortunate in
that his desire to improve and his ability to work hard
have not left him despite the avalanche of money that
has come his way.*

*If you ever watch Langer practising during a
tournament you will not see - as so often happens - an
aimless exercise, a golfer merely posing on the putting
green because he has a few hours to kill. One of Langer's
strengths is that he rarely does anything without there
being some purpose to it. He is a rather serious man
although not without humour. Certainly he has the
ability to laugh at himself and this, I always feel, is a
good sign. He grins readily at jokes even if he does not
crack many himself. He is utterly loyal and combines
an instinctive honesty with a natural discretion. He
forgives weaknesses in others far swifter than he ever
forgives his own faults.*

*Quiet and unassuming, his shy exterior sometimes
gives the impression that he is lacking passion.
Nothing could be further from the truth. It is just that
Langer is less overtly demonstrative than some sportsmen. He is a hard man in the sense that he considers
things carefully and once his mind is made up he is a
difficult man to budge. But he also would be a good man
to have alongside you when your back is against the
wall. After spending many hours with him unravelling
his life story I can say one thing for certain about
Bernhard Langer - he is a nice guy. It is, I think, a
conclusion he will appreciate more than offering a
batch of superlatives about his golf game.*

Doing this book has brought me much pleasure. It is an
interesting exercise to reflect on one's life. Even though
I hope I have much of mine yet to live, I have been able
to zero in on those important times, on the good, the bad

and the indifferent. And the more I consider the past, the more I relish the future. There is so much left to accomplish, so many ambitions to fulfil.

I have won many tournaments in many different countries. I have experienced the joy of a major victory in the US Masters, the thrill of my first big win in England in the Dunlop Masters and I have shared the ecstasy of two Ryder Cup triumphs. There has been the despair of watching my putting stroke all but disintegrate before my eyes and then the satisfaction of recovering from this ordeal - not once, but twice.

Over the years I have been to many fabulous places because of golf and I have met, and made friends with, some terrific people. I have worked very hard and I have had some luck when I needed it. There was, for example, my first experience of playing in the German National as a nervous teenager. My partner on the first tee of the first day was an experienced amateur who was considerably older than me. When I sliced my tee shot into the trees he walked over to me, put a fatherly arm round my shoulder and told me I should calm down and just try to enjoy it. I chipped my ball out of the trees and then holed a full eight iron for a birdie three. I don't know who laughed more, him or me.

Luck like that does not come every day but in golf, as in life, we must learn to live with whatever is thrown against us. I have had very little luck, for example, in the British Open. Twice in the eighties I have been second and several times I have figured strongly in the competition but always something goes wrong. In 1981 when I was runner-up to Bill Rogers at Royal St George's I was not really ready to win it. Back then it was a matter of hanging on, of clutching what I could while my nerves jangled in the wind. In 1984 I was vying with Seve and Tom Watson for the title at St Andrews. This time I was ready but I could not make a putt that final day, and finished tied for second spot with Watson while Seve did his matador bit on the final green.

Perhaps I want the Open Championship too much so that I try just that little bit too hard and my concentration starts to falter because of the extra pressure I put on myself. What I know for certain is that my best ever chance of victory came in 1985, the year that Sandy Lyle finished up crossing his fingers and everything else as he waited to see if anyone in the remaining groups could catch or equal his score at Royal St George's.

The last pair out that day was made up of myself and Australian David Graham. I had begun that last round full of optimism. All week I had played well and my confidence was tremendously high as I contemplated adding the Open title to my US Masters victory achieved just three months earlier. Surely, I believed, this was to be my time. As usual my destiny lay in my own hands and, as usual in the Open, those hands did not quite do the job for me. I was tied with Graham – we had a three-shot lead – but when I missed a short putt on the first green for bogey, all that confidence that had danced through my body over the earlier days began to evaporate like rainwater in a desert sun.

By the time I came to the last hole I needed a birdie three to tie Sandy and force a play-off. My approach shot was strong and a little to the right of the flag so that it bounced through to nestle in the long grass. I then hit a pitch out of the rough that honestly ranks with any of the shots I've ever played. This was no time to worry about getting up and down in two shots; this was all about making that one shot to try to achieve a lifetime's ambition. For one brief glorious moment as the ball spun in the bright, sunlit air I thought I had just created my own special piece of magic. The ball seemed destined for the hole and I could feel the excitement welling up inside my body like a fountain of joy.

But, of course, the ball did not go into the hole. Instead it grazed the flag and rolled a few feet past. I felt terribly deflated. The disappointment inside me was bleak because I knew that I had thrown away my chance. Not in that one shot but over the preceding holes. If I had shot even 73 that final day then I would be an Open champion already. Looking back I cannot quite fathom out why I did not score at least as well as that.

It was at the same Championship that the Great Sweater Scandal broke. There were even a few people who thought the incident had put me off my game so much that it alone accounts for the weak way I played on the final day. It would be nice to clutch such an excuse to my chest - along with the sweater - but it would not be true.

What happened was that I had just signed up to represent Boss and I had a whole selection of clothes to wear for the Open. On that final day I chose to wear a shade of red as I had done to some effect at Augusta in April that year. As far as choosing my sweater was concerned, I merely looked at the posse of wool I had in my room and picked out a red pullover. I don't think I even bothered to look at it properly.

Then, after starting the round in shirtsleeves, the weather turned cool and I reached into my bag and put on the sweater. Unknown to me but clearly visible to the watching millions on television - a group that included members of the Royal and Ancient Championship Committee - was the single word BOSS emblazoned on the back of the sweater in letters large enough to be read by a half-blind man at the other end of the course. It was not exactly subtle advertising for my sponsor - but it was an innocent gaffe.

I understand that several BBC cameramen went

cross-eyed trying to figure out angles whereby they could take a picture of me playing a shot but not show the back of the sweater. Personally, I think it is quite funny but one or two people took it very seriously. The R and A, however, were their usual laid-back and polite selves and it was quietly pointed out to me that if it happened again then I would simply not appear on television.

As it would be difficult for everyone if the winner of the Open Championship was not actually seen winning the trophy on television, I intend to follow this piece of advice. I also intend to win the Open Championship. And I believe that one day I will do just that. In fact, I hope to do it more than once although that might be a little bit greedy. If absolutely necessary, I'll settle for one.

It is just a matter of time. And effort. And graft. And then all I need is that little bit of luck. It is the same in the other majors. I expect to win several more titles before I am through. Nowadays I judge myself by the majors because these are the ones that count, the trophies that offer at least a little immortality to us otherwise ordinary human beings.

My ambition is to win each of the four major titles at least once. It is not, I believe, an outrageous target. I know that I shall try to do it my way by playing as well as I can and by leaving little to chance. It is an attitude that over the years has earned me a reputation as a slow player. It is a charge I must, to a certain extent, accept. But not totally. I am meticulous – or I try to be – when I am playing golf simply because there is rarely a second chance and just one bad shot, one terrible misjudgement of pace or yardage can wreck everything.

Also I see little point in rushing a shot and then waiting on the next tee which is frequently the prospect facing me as a player week in, week out. A few years ago

I was fined 500 dollars for slow play during the Tournament Players' Championship in America. After 27 holes I was playing very well. In fact I was 10 under par when the official warned my group that we were falling behind. He told me that I had been timed over three shots and taken more than 45 seconds on each occasion to hit the ball. I started trying to hurry my game and I did get quicker. I also got worse and that meant I got slower. The simple truth is that if you hit the ball into trouble then you take more time to get out of that trouble. Result: slow play.

So I ruined my score and because I was having to hit the ball more often - if quicker - our actual pace of play got even slower. It was a mistake I will not make again. Another lesson learned. You see, I have an almost physical need to win now and then. It is a feeling I feed off and thrive on. I would rather win a title and then do nothing for several weeks than have a string of top 10 finishes. Maybe I would earn more money that way but the real reward, the satisfaction that comes with victory, would not be there. I would also rather win one major than 10 other tournaments because the real joy dances in each of those four historic titles.

They say it takes special nerve to win a tournament and even more nerve to succeed in a major. Critics point to such and such a player and state blandly that he 'doesn't have enough bottle' to win. In the States they talk about certain players 'taking the gas'. Well, it is all relative. As far as I am concerned every player who comes on the Tour has nerve. If they did not then they would opt for an easier and certainly a more predictable way of earning a living.

No matter how good a player is, how brilliant his form, none of us knows what the next week, the following year, may bring. In 1985, for example, I was nothing special in the opening two rounds of most tournaments but outstanding over the last 36 holes. In 1987 I frequently played excellently over the first 36 holes and then slumped. Yet in the same year I won the PGA Championship with a record score and followed that up with victory in the Irish Open. Just another example of golf's whimsical nature I suppose.

Yet for all of us, whether we are towards the top of the heap or nearer the bottom, golf offers each of us a wonderful way of living our lives. Of course it is work to me but I enjoy it and it means that I have made my hobby my business. Every day I go to my 'office' and I have fun and that is not true for most workers. Some days, however, it is more fun than others. And some days are really bleak.

One of the bleakest days of my life came early in 1988 when my long-suffering back really started to give me trouble. Like a lot of golfers I have suffered from back problems for many years. It is part and parcel of the game. The unnatural contortions we require our bodies to perform thousands of times a year in order to hit the ball invariably means trouble for each and every one of us.

Ironically, my own back problems were not started by my urgent enthusiasm for golf but because the German Air Force felt that marching across 10 miles of open countryside in freezing conditions while wearing a backpack was a good idea.

After I had been on the European Tour for one year I received my call-up papers for the German Air Force. My National Service was to begin promptly on 1 January 1977. The first three months were spent doing basic training with the other lads. After that I was to be posted to a special company made up of sportsmen and life was to become much easier. These first three months, however, were hell. I hated every minute of it.

Just a few weeks after joining I was ordered to take

part in a 10-mile march in freezing conditions. Like the others I had a backpack that weighed between 20 and 30 pounds and a rifle that grew heavier by the yard. Although it was freezing, the exertion of marching quickly had us sweating profusely. Eventually we stopped to have something to eat by the roadside. It was then, while we were halfway through our meal, that an officer shouted out that 'enemy aircraft were coming in' and we had to take immediate cover by diving headlong into the snow. As I hit the snow my pack banged into my back like a small but effective sledgehammer. It hurt but there was no time to explain this to anyone. Instead, I had to get back on to my feet and complete the march.

That evening I still felt some pain but the next morning I could hardly get out of bed. Instead of marching again I was sent to a hospital where I received heat treatment, was hung upside down and massaged. In all I was in hospital two and a half weeks before returning to my unit. Although I continued to have the occasional painful twinge, I thought little more about it for the rest of my time in the Air Force.

Two months later, I was posted to this special company made up of weightlifters, athletes and cyclists. I was the only golfer in it but, like everyone else, I was allowed to practise my sport for most of the day for the next 12 months. It only took a letter from the German Golf Federation or the German P G A requesting my presence in a tournament to secure my release and, meanwhile, I was living a reasonable life.

I was posted closer to my home so that I spent most nights in my own bed. In the entire 12 months after basic training I slept for no more than 30 nights in the barracks. But I still hated it. The mindless attempt to instil a curious sort of immediate obedience and discipline seemed to me to be unnecessary. It was the usual story of breaking down an individual's resistance until he became almost robotic and I detested it as did all the other young men I had joined with. They would order you to clean your boots and then, just as you had polished them to a perfect shine, some fool in charge would wipe dirt over them and order you to clean them again. No wonder most of the lads stifled their frustration by getting drunk at night after 12 hours of this sort of nonsense. I couldn't wait to get out of it and away from the anti-aircraft battery I was supposed to be able to operate.

The Air Force, however, have never forgotten me. Several times since they have tried to call me up to spend a few weeks sharpening up my so-called skills. Each time I have managed to avoid going back into uniform because of an important tournament clashing with their dates. Last time, for example, they wanted me to report back during the week of the British Open in 1983. Great military planning, don't you think?

One legacy of my Air Force days, however, has remained with me – my injured back. Since 1977 it has caused me real problems only rarely. Until January and February of 1988. In those months I reached a plateau of pain and discomfort that I had never known before and which I wish never to encounter again. To be honest, I was frightened. Badly frightened.

Medically, the condition is simple enough to explain. I have a stress fracture, two bulging discs and degenerating disc disease. It sounds as though I am about to fall apart. Hopefully this is not the case. Yet even though reports of my demise were, as Mark Twain once put it, 'somewhat exaggerated', there is equally no point trying to dilute the serious nature of the problem. When it hurts, it hurts a lot.

There have been times when I have had to crawl out of bed, times when the pain has doubled me up and kept me that way for most, if not all, of the day. Even determination cannot get me on to the golf course when this happens. At these times I worry not just about whether I can go on playing golf but whether I will be able to lead a normal life.

At one stage I was forced, reluctantly, to contemplate surgery. I say reluctantly because there can always be mistakes with the surgeon's knife and the outcome is never really guaranteed one way or the other. Maybe I would be able to walk again without ever feeling pain but would I be able to subject my spine to the extreme stress of high-level competition?

No one could promise me this and so I am anxious to avoid surgery if at all possible. So far the signs are good. In spring of 1988 I spent two weeks in Germany having my back treated by a superb team that consisted of a physiotherapist, a chiropractor and an orthopedic doctor. Each worked in close cooperation with the other, each knew what the other was doing and why. The result has been a fantastic, almost unbelieveable improvement.

My worry was that I would begin to compensate for the back pain so that other parts of my body would be affected. That worry seems now to have passed. The truth is that we were never meant to walk upright in the first place. Swinging a golf club is only adding pressure to an earlier mistake but, so far, it seems as though my playing career is no longer facing the threat of a premature end. If, however, such a thing were to happen it would no longer mean the absolute end of my world. There would be a tremendous void of course, but my life - and its priorities - have changed in the last few years.

When I started out it was at least a million to one shot that I would achieve anything of note in golf. Yet my background, the very thing that seemed set against me, has proved in the final analysis to be my inspiration. It was always a big dream to build my own house in

Anhausen. I had watched my father work very hard, observed my mother labour on my uncle's farm, and graft as a cleaning lady and as a waitress. I came from a family with little to show in material terms and I was hungry for those things. But I also came from a family where there was much love and a great deal of support. My story is their story too.

My little village is a special place. The people are special, they stick together and they help each other when the going gets tough. There is love as well as quaintness in this area. In 1985 when I returned home as Masters champion I was met at the station and taken by car not to my home but to the Mayor's office. There, waiting for me, was a horsedrawn carriage and I was taken on a marvellous procession through Anhausen.

It was a complete – and delightful – surprise and as I passed along all those familiar streets and acknowledged the applause of people I had known all my life, I knew true happiness. Not only because I had returned a champion from America but because my friends and relatives in Anhausen took such obvious joy in my achievement. My uncle had turned one of his barns into a hall and there we drank and ate and toasted victory in Augusta. Such days cannot be bought, only treasured.

It is the same with my own family now. Not so long ago I would have said I loved golf more than anything else apart from God. This is no longer the case. My wife and daughter mean more to me than the game that has made my name. Winning the U S Masters was fantastic but seeing my daughter for the first time was a far greater thrill.

I remember my first coach, Heinz Fehring, telling me that I should beware of becoming a one-dimensional man, that I must not be possessed by golf. He said that if I was possessed then, though I might win a few more trophies and some extra money, I would lose out on something far more important. Heinz is absolutely right. Golf is a great game – but the greatest game of all is life itself.

In some ways, golf is a metaphor for life. It tends to strike you down just when you are beginning to believe you have mastered it. There have been many examples of this in my career but allow me to leave you with just one. In 1985 I played in the European Open at Sunningdale. It was an event I was to win but as I played the second hole in the opening round, victory was, for once, the last thing on my mind.

I had hit a good drive but then pushed my approach shot to the right and into some heather just 10 yards from the green. The ball was sitting up nicely. And it was still sitting up nicely after my first shot. I had missed it. So I swung again and once more failed to touch the ball. I was embarrassed naturally, but I also could not help laughing. Here I was, a top golfer, and I had twice failed to make contact with the ball.

That is golf – and that is life. To begin a book with victory in the U S Masters and end it with two air shots seems to me to be just about right...

Career statistics

Date of birth: 27 August 1957
Turned professional: 1972
Low round: 62 – Benson and Hedges Spanish Open 1984
Sony World Ranking in 1988: 3
Team Events: Ryder Cup – 1981, 1983, 1985, 1987
                Hennessey Cognac Cup – 1976, 1978, 1980, 1982 (captain)
                World Cup – 1976, 1977, 1978, 1979, 1980
                Kirin Cup – 1985, 1986, 1987 (captain each year)

Tournament victories:

PGA European Tour

1980 Dunlop Masters
1981 German Open; Bob Hope British Classic
1982 Lufthansa German Open
1983 Italian Open; Glasgow Golf Classic; St Mellion Timeshare Tournament Players' Championship
1984 Peugeot French Open; KLM Dutch Open; Carrolls Irish Open; Benson and Hedges Spanish Open
1985 Lufthansa German Open; Panasonic European Open
1986 German Open; Lancôme Trophy (tied)
1987 Whyte and Mackay PGA Championship; Carrolls Irish Open
1988 (to date) Epson Grand Prix of Europe Matchplay Championship

Other tournament victories:

1979 German Close Pro Championship; Cacharel Under-25's Championship
1980 Colombian Open

1983 Johnnie Walker Tournament; Casio World Open (Japan)

1985 Australian Masters; US Masters; Sea Pines Heritage Classic (U S); Sun City Invitational

European tour earnings (to date):

Year	Order of Merit	Prize money
1976	90	£2130
1977	—	£691
1978	40	£7006
1979	56	£7972
1980	9	£32,395
1981	1	£95,991
1982	6	£48,008
1983	3	£83,605
1984	1	£160,883
1985	2	£142,124
1986	—	£125,801
1987	5	£164,821
1988 (so far)		£50,000
	Total:	£921, 507

US Tour Official Earnings:

Year	Money List	Prize money (dollars)
1984	75	82,465
1985	13	271,044
1986	10	379,800
1987	23	366,430
	Total:	1,099,739

Miscellaneous:

Harry Vardon Trophy (top player in Europe) – 1981, 1984

European Tour Stats Leader – 1983 sand saves (71%)

1984 putts per round (28.84)

1985 greens in regulation (72%)

Index